Focus on History

D1387493

The Years of Napoleon

C. J. Hunt, B.Sc. (Econ.)
and
G. A. Embleton

ALMARK PUBLISHING CO. LTD., LONDON

First published—December 1972

ISBN 0 85524 105 5 (hard cover edition)
ISBN 0 85524 106 3 (paper covered edition)

Printed in Great Britain by
Vale Press Ltd., Mitcham, Surrey CR4 4HR
for the publishers, Almark Publishing Co. Ltd.,
270 Burlington Road, New Malden,
Surrey KT3 4NL, England.

Introduction

ONLY relatively rarely does a single man almost completely dominate the events of his time. Hitler in the 20th century is the nearest we can get in living memory to a man with comparable power and influence to Napoleon. Both men had ambitions to dominate the world, both were influenced by major social changes in their formative years, both were opportunists, and both nearly succeeded in their aims but over-stretched their resources and talents to bring spectacular and dramatic endings to their respective régimes.

The impact of Napoleon was, perhaps, even greater, relative to his times than Hitler. The poor communications of the day, and the less well-knit societies of Europe made it easier to terrorise and subjugate the nations which fell under Napoleon's ruthless will. Similarly the fragmented forces which opposed Napoleon took much longer to muster their strength and organise their attempts to crush the French emperor.

The career of Napoleon was long and eventful and is recorded already in many detailed biographies. This book is not intended to be a biography, but rather it seeks to provide a basis for study of Napoleon's life and career, set against the events which he directly influenced. It should act as an introduction to the subject for the interested layman, the student, or the military enthusiast. The appendices give a chronology of important dates and concurrent events in Napoleon's time, plus some suggested books for further study. Because Napoleon was a military man using military means to impose his will, the Napoleonic age is inevitably linked with armies and warfare. A complete section of this book is devoted to the soldiers and armies of the period with examples of the uniforms, equipment, and types of soldier and tactics. Again this is of an introductory nature for the subject of Napoleonic armies and warfare alone is immense and many specialist volumes are available for further study of this aspect of the period.

Extensive use has been made of contemporary and near-contemporary prints and engravings to illustrate this book in addition to the original artwork done specially for the volume. For the loan of engravings dating back to 1840 or earlier the authors are grateful to David Nash. Other old illustrations are from the authors' own collections.

CONTENTS

1: An Opportunity is Taken, 1789-1793

IN July 1789 the people of Paris took to the streets, and the world of today began—the world of protest and direct action, of rival political factions and fervours, of the growing importance of the 'man in the street' and the public opinion he expresses, of ever-increasing criticism and challenge to almost everything in what was once called 'the established order'. On July 14 the fortress-prison of the Bastille fell, stormed by the Paris mob; and though at its fall only a handful of prisoners crawled forth into the light of day, yet it was so hated as the grim outward symbol of tyranny, that its destruction came to be regarded as a new dawn. The day that followed did not see the solution of the problem of Liberty and Authority (that problem plagues mankind still), but at least it was henceforth out in the open, and arbitrary rule everywhere would now be challenged.

The Revolution could have begun elsewhere in Europe: the grievances that provoked it (despotic and discriminatory rule, lack of redress through legal channels or electoral process, heavy taxation and downright hunger), were not peculiar to France at the time; but the volatile character of the French, and the corruption and incompetence that increasingly marked the country's leadership and ruling classes, made revolution both inevitable and more likely to succeed. Further, a whole series of writers and philosophers had created a situation where change was in the air; not that they were democrats or crude agitators as we understand the terms today, but they had on the academic level explored the basis for a more natural, or just, or humane and reasonable society.

So the new masters took over, at first on a wave of wild enthusiasm and reforming zeal. In August, the Constituent Assembly began making changes some of which may seem trivial or absurd in the light of today, though it is rarely right to judge one age by the standards of another. However, though we may smile at the self-conscious use of the title Citizen for all and sundry, at the regard for the red cap of the Revolution and the new almanac, some of the changes were just and practical and have endured without substantial modification ever since—notably the re-distribution of the land taken from nobility and church.

However, it seems that revolutions, initiating change by force instead of by natural growth, either do more than or less than was intended. As the years that followed '89 brought more problems than solutions, so the lack of unity and agreement among the new political leaders became clearer, and the Revolution followed its course from crisis to crisis,

The House where Napoleon was born, 1769, in Ajaccio. The original house was burnt in 1793, in local Corsican 'troubles', but was quickly restored by Napoleon's mother, and is now kept as a Napoleon Museum.

its negative or destructive side all the time increasing as one political leader, clique or party attempted to solve the constitutional issues by controlling the Assembly and discrediting all rivals. A new and most damning accusation could now be made against one's political adversaries —'an enemy of the people', or 'of the Revolution' and it had (and has) a sinister ring. In the autumn of '89 the Royal family had been forced back to Paris from Versailles; rights and privileges were stripped from the nobility (many of whom managed to get away), and the Church itself came under censure, as a pillar of the old order (l'ancien régime). The death in 1791 of Mirabeau, a statesman-like leader of the Assembly, put an end to any possibility of a constitutional monarchy, and as power then passed from one demagogue to another, the fair slogan 'Liberty, Equality, Fraternity' was used to cover or excuse all kinds of excesses.

This tended to discredit the Revolution, both in France itself (where pockets of sympathy for royalist and aristocrat still lingered in the west and south), and also abroad (as in England, where the news of 1789 had at first been welcomed). Far from checking excesses, this antagonism and the advance of Prussian troops into eastern France only stoked the fires of excitement and revolutionary ardour still further; and in the autumn of '92 the National Convention (replacing the Legislative Assembly) proclaimed a republic and put King Louis XVI on trial. With the party of extreme republican views (the Jacobins) in power, the King (and soon afterwards his Queen, Marie-Antoinette) were beheaded by guillotine. Many local uprisings started in France and a state of war developed with the rest of western Europe where governments felt their

6

territory and their political ideas threatened by the fanatical zeal of the new revolutionary French army, with panic, insecurity and frustration at the dis-array of government replacing the Rule of Reason, which the politicians at Paris claimed to admire, there began in 1793 the terrible Reign of Terror. This period of mainly wanton and senseless beheading, when an average of up to thirty a day went to the guillotine on trumpery charges or on mere suspicion, only came to an end when Robespierre, head of the Revolutionary Tribunal, was himself executed in July '94, just as he had removed Danton a few months before.

Events had got really out of hand. Charge and counter-charge, plot and counterplot, for months in '94 produced a steady procession of tumbrils rattling over the cobbled streets of Paris towards the place of execution, conveying their pathetic or wretched load to swell the evergrowing harvest of blood and vengeance: 'aristos', discredited politicians and any unfortunates on whom the charge of treachery to the Revolution could be pinned. Yet even as the terrible toll mounted, and the blood-lust rose to fever-heat; even as the Paris mob grew to accept the deadly work as entertainment and spectacle, and the good dames from the back streets reputedly took their knitting to the foot of the guillotine, greeting each fresh despatch with shrieks and ribald comment, never dropping a stitch but changing their pattern, thus forming a record for posterity of how many people were guillotined; even at the height of the frenzied drama, he who was to prove ultimately the chief character had not emerged, but like an actor was waiting in the wings for his cue.

It might have surprised the Paris politicians if they could have known that Napoleon Bonaparte (who had graduated from the Military College of this very city of Paris, and who had as a young commander of artillery been recently promoted to high rank in the republican army attempting to free the naval harbour of Toulon from the British) was to become the 'residual legatee' of the revolutionary and republican changes after 1789. Toulon was his opportunity. It proved a welcome victory for the government, it gained Napoleon promotion and helped to shape his ambition.

Napoleon Bonaparte was a Corsican, born in Ajaccio into one of the island's respected families, significantly enough in 1769, just after the incorporation of Corsica (hitherto an appendage of Genoa) into France.

Napoleon spent his childhood at Ajaccio, Corsica, shown in this contemporary print as it was in Napoleon's time. The citadel is to the left, the town to the right. The young Napoleon was taken to France at the age of nine.

Educated at Brienne and in Paris, he proved a good military student, with an appetite for historical and geographical facts, a hard worker, but quiet and self-contained to the point of taciturnity. He might have become the leader of a liberation movement in his native Corsica, but decided against further involvement when the status of the island was raised in the 'new France'. He showed enthusiasm for the Revolution in its early days, but, being in Paris in the summer of 1792, he saw more than one instance of mob-rule and massacre. After seven years in the army, he had developed soldierly instincts for discipline and order; but apart from an occasional outburst he kept his disillusioned thoughts to himself, just accepting the Revolution and, as many did, quietly making up his mind to use for personal advancement any opportunities that would surely occur in the developing situation. Perhaps from this time (1792-3) one can see his ambition taking definite shape. It is not always a fruitful exercise to speculate on the role of 'great men' in history—how far they make history and how far history makes them—but certainly a possible formula for success is to observe the trend of events and opinions, decide which 'band-wagon' one might go forward on most successfully, and then use the position of power so gained actually to guide or manipulate events and circumstances to one's liking. There is also the factor of sheer chance, and one has to admit that on more than one occasion there was a lucky turn of events to help the young Corsican along. But be that as it may, he was destined to dominate, or over-shadow, the life of his country and indeed of all Europe for the next twenty years, and even indirectly for much longer. For though 'the Age of Napoleon' may be said to finish with his final defeat at Waterloo, in a sense it continued long after, so great was his personal impact, the forceful presentation of his case in his writings in exile, and the 'legend' associated with his name.

2: Building a Reputation, 1794-1797

FOR his energy, determination and military skill displayed at Toulon, Napoleon was promoted to brigadier-general by a grateful government, and from now on his story takes on some of the character of a fast-moving novel. A quick trip to Genoa in the spring of 1794 gave him the geographical and military information that he needed for planning a campaign. By summer, however, he was in prison under suspicion of complicity with the now discredited tyrant Robespierre; but as he had wisely avoided close contact with Paris there was no evidence to implicate him and he was soon released, restored to rank, and was back in the field thwarting an Austrian attempt to cut French communications with northern Italy; for there was a continental coalition threatening the young republic at several points.

Wanting to lead an Italian campaign against the Austrians established in the north, Napoleon was disappointed at being given an infantry command against royalist insurgents in the west. He demurred, went to Paris and won over the government to supporting his plans for northern Italy, only to lose the support of his backers in the treacherous political reefs and shoals, and by September '95 was once more threatened with loss of rank.

However, luck took a hand: the National Convention in Paris, in spite of a new constitution and a fresh start after the Terror, was seen

Bonaparte orders the cannon to fire on the insurgents, October 5, 1795. An insurrection which threatened the authority of the Convention was put down promptly by the young commander of artillery, with cannon hastily brought by Murat from the nearest camp. This was the occasion of the oft-quoted 'whiff of grapeshot'.

Napoleon at Arcola, November, 1796. This action against the Austrians has perhaps received more publicity than other French victories in the north Italian campaign, as in the course of it, at a critical point, the eager young commander himself seized the banner and had to be restrained from leading the way across the bridge which was being stubbornly defended by a Croatian battalion. This incident has inspired several painters. Napoleon was probably saved from death by being pushed into the water in the confusion at the bridge!

to be manoeuvring to keep its hold on the Legislative Assembly. Feeling ran high, but the insurrection was nipped in the bud by the intervention of Napoleon's artillery units under Murat. The general himself took personal charge of the short sharp spell of street fighting, astonishing everybody by his vigour and his confident appraisal of the situation. This incident is usually referred to as the 'whiff of grapeshot' as Napoleon is supposed to have remarked that a whiff of grapeshot would soon cure the crowd's grievances. For thus saving the government and preserving national unity under the revolutionary settlement, General Bonaparte appeared as patriot, champion of equality, and strong man ensuring law and order. His reward was inevitable and immediate—command of the Army of the Interior. In modern jargon, he was 'well on the way'.

Now, as if confirming this stage of his fortunes in its guise of romantic novel, a woman entered his life. He fell violently in love with the distinguished and gracious Josephine Beauharnais, young widow of a Republican army general. Though not himself perhaps very romantic physically, being short, sallow, and of brooding appearance, Napoleon certainly impressed Josephine by his ardour and courage, and in March 1796 they were married. Two days before, Napoleon's wish, the Italian command, had been granted.

By now, the coalition of autocratic powers had crumbled, and the successful republican French army was no longer a rabble, but a better equipped and well-officered force, animated by enthusiasm for France and its republican ideals, and willing to risk casualties beyond the numbers customary in the conventional struggles of the 18th century fought out largely by mercenaries. It carried the French tricolour into the Low Countries, the Rhineland, and south-east into hitherto Italian territory, Nice and Savoy. Political unification of Italy was still more than half a century away, and most of the populous north, with its fine farmland and numerous ancient cities, was either under Austrian domination,

The young Napoleon in 1796 as General of the Interior, from a contemporary portrait by Guérin.

or else in Sardinia and Piedmont, or in the ancient city-state of Venice. Austria was also the custodian of what is now Belgium, and so had most interest in thwarting the French. Britain was the other main interested party, for maritime and commercial reasons, but in the then state of the French at sea there could be little contact between them. So Napoleon went all out for a vigorous campaign against the Austrians in northern Italy, concentrating first on separating them from their Sardinian allies and then on taking the strongly held city of Mantua and on smashing the series of Austrian armies sent to its relief. He achieved this in a string of victories brilliantly executed in double quick time.

Apart from the superior numbers of the Austrians, everything was in Napoleon's favour: the buoyant enthusiasm of his troops, the quality of the experienced veteran commanders who accepted his generalship (Augereau, Masséna and Berthier), the mistakes and obstinacy of the Austrians (who split their forces), the tactical brilliance of Napoleon himself in improvising and in making the best use of all arms (artillery, cavalry, infantry and support units), and the fact that he possessed weapons unknown to earlier times. The improved musket, the light field gun, horse artillery, were not his invention, but for the first time he showed how flexible by their means military operations could be, especially when based on a prior knowledge, by map or reconnaissance, of the geographical lie of the land. The smoke and din of the battlefield remained, but with a new feature in mobility and lightning switches master-minded by one who may have been brought up as an artilleryman, but now showed himself as a military genius. Perhaps the Austrians cannot be blamed for repeated defeat: Napoleon gave them little time to adjust to the new style of fighting where a whole nation was in arms from the women and children at home making bandages to practically the entire youth of a nation fighting in the 'front line', unlike the 'professional' armies of the rest of the European countries where only the army fought while the rest of the country went about its normal business.

This in a nutshell is the difference between the two sides of the Napoleonic wars: on the one hand a nation convinced of its own destiny united under the leadership of one man, on the other the old feudal monarchies co-operating in a bid to crush an upstart but going about things in the old way of letting the army get on with the business in the time honoured fashion, with, in many cases, incompetent commanders

Napoleon's troops (right) move forward to attack Castiglione. The defending Austrian troops are on the hillside to the left.

who only held their posts because of their noble birth. It is little wonder then that these armies were beaten all along the line.

A victory at Montenotte in the hinterland of Genoa forced the separation of the Austrians (who were also defeated at Dego), from their Sardinian and Piedmontese allies, who suffered reverses at Millesimo, Ceva and Mondovi. Napoleon quickly followed the retreating Austrians across the Lombardy Plain, entering Milan in triumph in mid-May after forcing the crossing of the Adda at Lodi. (A new feature in warfare was now visible: armies had often 'lived off the land,' and individual soldiers were apt to plunder; but the 'contributions' which Napoleon exacted from conquered territories were more than considerable, in this land of art treasures!) Further pursuit of the Austrians brought the French to the line of the Mincio and then to the Adige, commanding the route north across the Alps; and this was safely open to them once Mantua had fallen, as a result of hard fighting and another string of victories against stubborn opponents at Lonato, Castiglione, Roveredo, Bassano, Arcola, Rivoli and the river Tagliamento.

Successes like these did not turn Napoleon's head however, but just confirmed him in a belief in himself. He was not unmindful of the political and psychological side of war: he was eloquent enough to make telling emotive appeals to his men, to gain the confidence of officers far older and more experienced than himself, to project his own energy, resolve and courage into the whole army (and, after results, into the French nation, as nothing succeeds like success), to encourage Italian aspirations towards freedom and democracy, to give solemn warning to the antagonistic Pope without alienating Catholic opinion, and to get his way with his own government. Whatever his ultimate aim, here was not just a demagogue, but a statesman, not just a brilliant general, but a national hero.

RIGHT: the Revolution left the regular French Army in ruins, the majority of officers had been Royalists and these, with many soldiers and NCOs, had fled. The volunteer army—the National Guard—was enthusiastic, but lacked arms, discipline and training. In 1793 France was invaded by the armies of Prussia and Austria. To counter this threat the organization of the French army was reformed and 209 Demi-Brigades of Infantry and 42 of Light Infantry were formed. Each Demi-Brigade was formed by joining one battalion of white clad regular soldiers with two battalions of blue uniformed volunteers. The organization of the Cavalry and infantry remained as before. From the ragged, ill equipped and often half starved Demi-Brigades grew the army of Napoleon. . . .

Soldiers of
a Demi-Brigade
1793-1804

Peace was agreed to at Leoben in April '97 after a French thrust towards Vienna. In this, admittedly, a darker side to Napoleon's character can be seen: as an inducement to defeated Austria quickly to come to terms over losing Belgium and over the setting up in Lombardy of the Cisalpine Republic under French tutelage, the ancient republic of Venice was provoked and divided, and then handed over to Austria—cynical and arrogant perhaps, but only in accord with the times (and with the way Napoleon, in later years, graciously 'confirmed' Swiss peasants in the possession of high-level grazing rights enjoyed by their families for generations!) In the same spirit of 'realism' he had previously agreed to a Transpadane republic of various Italian cities, arbitrarily committing his government to the proposal. However, he was by now the master, not the servant; he lived in state near Milan, inaugurating the new republic, and surrounding himself with all the trappings of royalty; even in relaxation he showed his boundless energy and his ambition for himself, making no secret to his intimates that the mastery of France was his goal, though the time was not ripe. Everything played into his hands: another royalist threat to the Paris government in September '97 allowed him once again to 'save the Revolution' by a military coup d'état, and when the Peace of Campo Formio was officially signed with Austria in October, its terms dictated by Napoleon, he seemed supreme.

Flag of the 5th French Demi-Brigade. The 5th took part in the attack on the bridge at Arcola.

3: The Armies of the Napoleonic Wars

'The Grumblers'

The First Regiment of Foot Grenadiers of the Imperial Guard was truly
an 'elite' Regiment. They were picked men, over 5 ft 6 in (tall for
those days) and over 25 years of age. Loyalty to Napoleon and distinguished military service were essential. They guarded the Emperor's
person, and are almost as familiar a symbol of the French First Empire
as Napoleon himself. They received more pay, and better quality uniforms
and equipment than their comrades in the 'Line' and promotion could
mean officer rank in a Line Regiment. Their privileged position and
Napoleon's familiarity with them often allowed them to be outspoken—
hence their nickname, the Grumblers! But though they grumbled, they
never failed to follow: their loyalty was never in doubt. At the Battle of
Waterloo in 1815 the British Grenadier Guards won their title 'Grenadier'
(they were then the 1st Regiment of Foot Guards) because they defeated
the French Grenadiers of the Guard.

The French Imperial Guard

The Guard were the Emperor's crack troops, a formidable elite force of highly trained men consisting of all arms of the service, Cavalry, Infantry, Artillery and supporting units, almost an army within an army. Like a personal bodyguard on a huge scale they were usually kept in reserve by the Emperor to be sent in to strike the decisive blow. No effort was spared to build up morale. Guard troops had better pay, uniforms, and equipment, they outranked their counterparts in the rest of the army, who were often justifiably jealous!

The chasseurs-à-cheval (a regiment of light-horse dressed like hussars) were raised in 1800 from Napoleon's former bodyguard during the Egyptian campaign and a squadron always accompanied the Emperor on campaign, a detachment guarding him at all times. He sometimes wore their uniform, or that of the Guard Grenadiers.

In 1814 the Guard had expanded, the new units were known as the

Grenadier

Grenadiers were originally soldiers who were armed with hand grenades. They usually wore fur caps, so that when throwing grenades they could sling their muskets across their shoulders without knocking off the more usual wide brimmed hats. Grenades went out of general use in the 18th century but the Grenadiers remained as elite assault troops; most European armies had grenadier regiments or companies within the regiments during the Napoleonic wars, often distinguished by fur caps and grenade shaped badges.
RIGHT: Grenadier of 1st Regt of Foot Grenadiers, service dress, 1815.

'Young Guard', the veterans as the 'Old Guard', and numbered 112,500 men of all branches. Members of the Guard went into exile on Elba with Napoleon and formed the nucleus of his tiny army when he returned to France.

A bewhiskered veteran sergeant of the Old Guard teaches musket drill to a young recruit. More recruits can be seen drilling in the background. The recruits are wearing their soft forage caps (see page 23) worn usually when off-duty or when drilling. This is from a contemporary military print.

RIGHT: 1st Light Horse Lancers of the Guard, recruited from the Poles in 1807 and armed as lancers in 1809. Figures (from left) are lancer in overcoat, two mounted lancers, officer and trumpeter. Basic uniform was dark blue with crimson facings. Trumpeter had crimson trousers, white tunic, and crimson facings. Overcoat was light grey.

18

ABOVE: Chasseurs à Cheval (from left) trumpeter, officer, mounted trooper, trooper. Bottle green tunic (dolman) and red pelisse (jacket). Trumpeter had a sky blue dolman and white busby with blue/red plume. Trousers were buff. Other busbies were black with dark green/red plume. Cuffs were red, as were busby bags (both drawings from Hinton Hunt 'Prints Militaire' series).

The French Army

THE original army of Revolutionary France was frankly little more than an ill-disciplined rabble, unused to drill and training, poorly armed, and without proper uniform and boots. Their successes, won at great cost, were the result of their huge numbers and their enthusiasm and courage.

Universal military service not only provided numbers, however, but gave an opportunity for those of humble birth to rise from the ranks and achieve exalted positions in what Napoleon made an honoured profession. Helped by such men, and by some of the officers from pre-Revolutionary days, he soon succeeded in 'licking into shape' the troops who fought in northern Italy and along the Rhine. Retaining their patriotic and political fervour, they now had the advantages of proper training under professional officers, and the high morale that comes from success and faith in their commander.

Artillery

Artillery meant guns and gunners. Gunners were generally large fit men —it was heavy work manhandling guns—and a high standard of intelligence and training was necessary. Napoleon trained as an artilleryman and the French units were numerous and very skilfully used. A canonnier (gunner) of French Horse Artillery, 1810-1812, is shown.

By 1804, with the establishment of the Empire and the need for a large force to invade Britain (or to turn against Austria), Napoleon had a 'Grande Armée' of about 200,000, (130,000 infantry, 30,000 cavalry, 10,000 artillerymen with 400 cannon, and supporting services). This great army was divided up into 7 separate corps, each corps being an independent unit with its own due proportion of infantry, cavalry and artillery, commanded by Marshals like Ney and Soult. In addition there was a cavalry reserve under Murat, and of course the Imperial Guard, directly under the Emperor's orders.

Numbers, procedure and organisation did vary somewhat, but in general the basic unit was the battalion of six companies of about 140 men each. Three or four battalions would constitute a regiment, and two or three regiments a brigade. Two or three brigades made a division, and the autonomous corps was composed of one or more divisions.

Up to the time of Austerlitz, 1805, and Jena, 1806, Napoleon's army was basically French (and largely experienced veteran troops from earlier campaigns), helped by contributions from his south German 'satellites'. In later ventures, notably the Russian campaign, he 'diluted' his large armies with conscripts and levies from all over Europe.

In actual fighting, the conventional practice of sending long columns of men forward had been modified, before Napoleon's day, by sending out a lightly-armed screen of 'tirailleurs' or skirmishers, to distract the enemy, inflict a few

(continued on page 24)

Hussars

Hussars were light cavalry, famous for their traditional dash and courage. They are said to have originated from Hungarian cattle guards. The jacket (pelisse) worn hanging from the shoulder was the hussar's 'overcoat' in winter. French hussars generally wore a shako, only the élite companies having the fur cap, or busby. An officer of the 4th Hussar Regiment, 1810, is shown here.

21

GAE

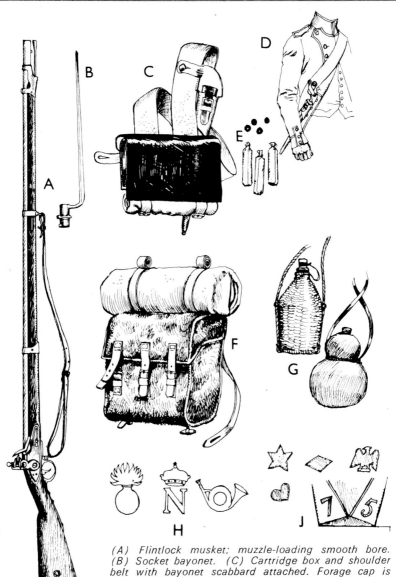

(A) Flintlock musket; muzzle-loading smooth bore.
(B) Socket bayonet. (C) Cartridge box and shoulder
belt with bayonet scabbard attached. Forage cap is
rolled and fastened under cartridge box. Grenadiers
wore sword and bayonet together on a separate
shoulder belt. (D) Method of wearing shoulder belt. (E) Paper cartridges
each containing powder for one charge, and a musket ball. (F) Cowhide
pack. Greatcoat rolled up, and fastened to top. (G) Water bottles were
improvised like these. (H) These ornaments denoted the company to
which the wearer belonged, grenadier, fusilier, or voltigeur respectively.
In brass they were worn on the cartridge box and in cloth on the turnbacks
of the coat tails; 1812-1815 period. (J) Before 1812 many other devices,
including the regimental number, could be seen in wear on the turnbacks.

The French Infantryman and his Equipment

ABOVE, LEFT TO RIGHT: The shako was a cylindrical felt or leather cap worn in some form or other by most European armies. The decorative cords were usually removed when on campaign. The coloured tuft which took many forms, generally denoted the wearer's company. Waterproof covers were issued or improvised to protect the shako when on campaign. For fatigues, off-duty wear, and sometimes drills and exercises, forage caps were worn; coloured piping and numerals denoted the wearer's unit. The tall cap shown is pre-1812, the round one (with flaps which would tie under the chin) dates from 1812 onwards.

RIGHT: A typical French line infantryman on campaign. Firewood and cooking utensils are fastened to his pack and rag is stuffed into the muzzle of his musket to keep out the rain. Cowhide pack contained clothes, spare shoes, brushes, and cleaning materials, personal belongings, sewing kit, rations, extra bottles were not usually issued to French troops, but many improvised their own from a wine bottle or a hollow gourd.

unexpected casualties, and so reduce the intensity of fire on the column. As an artilleryman, Napoleon made a great point of sending forward the guns alongside the infantry, concentrating fire from two or three angles on what he judged to be weak points, as a prelude to a break-through or an attack by heavy cavalry. His light cavalry and medium cavalry (dragoons) were for reconnaissance and maintaining communications, though the latter were armed to serve as infantry as well. In each battalion of foot soldiers, one company (usually agile men of slighter build) was typically 'light' infantry, and would share with its opposite numbers in other battalions the job of being 'tirailleurs': and a company of bigger, stronger men would be designated 'grenadiers' even though they no longer actually carried handgrenades.

The musket was the standard weapon of the infantryman; but while that might seem to indicate a high intensity of fire-power from any advancing column, whether on a single or a double company front, it must be remembered that only the front three ranks could really fire their weapons effectively. Bayonet-fighting was not typical of the Napoleonic period, and the problem of long baggage and supply columns was less important with French armies since they were trained to live off the country.

Lancer

The Lance was the traditional weapon of the Polish cavalry, and Napoleon, very impressed with the Polish lancers, adopted them into his guard. Other regiments armed with a lance were raised and were extremely successful in battle. Most European armies had regiments of lancers; Britain equipped four in 1816. In Germany they were called 'Uhlans'. The traditional Polish cap, also adopted by other nations, was called a 'Schapka'. A lancer of the French 2nd Guard Lancer Regiment is shown.

24

Russia and its Army

THE process of nation-building on the great plains stretching east to the Urals had been subject from early times to set-backs and interuptions, such as the great Mongol and Tartar invasion of the early thirteenth century, and incessant rivalry with Poland, Lithuania and the Cossacks. From among many small territories, Moscow emerged as the leading centre, and, under the house of Romanov from the early seventeenth century, the vast land was hammered into the semblance of a nation-state, with one religion dominant (the Greek Orthodox), and one racial group (the Russian Slavs) numerous enough to foster unity.

A privileged nobility, supported by large estates and the work of humble cultivators, exercised power as ministers, officials and military leaders, and their influence (sometimes deliberate, sometimes not) acted as a brake on any real progress or reform on m o d e r n lines. In fact, the status of the peasantry declined, and after 1648 they were little better than serfs. Even the rule of relatively forward-looking despots like Peter the Great and Catherine II brought little benefit to the people at large, though they strengthened the machinery of state. Thus the vast territory inherited in 1801 by the young Czar Alexander I. was not on a par with other great

Dragoon

Dragoons were originally mounted infantrymen, armed and trained as foot soldiers but mounted for mobility. By 1800 the dragoons of most armies had become heavy cavalry, although sometimes serving on foot. For infantry action they were armed with muskets and bayonets. They were often used for escort, patrol, and police duties. The illustration shows a member of Russian Dragoon Regiment Pereaslavski, 1812.

powers in efficiency and organisation: the countryside was backward, industry rudimentary, communications poor, and the absence of any democratic institutions deprived the state of potential talent.

Nevertheless, the huge man-power of the army put Russia among the ranks of emerging 'powers'. (The Czar had 200,000 men in 3 armies in 1812). Ordinary infantry, simply termed musketeers, were in regiments of 3 battalions—300 to 800 men each, and split into 1 grenadier company and 3 musketeer companies. One battalion of each three was a garrison or reserve battalion, but all grenadier companies could be merged to act in the field. Light Jäger regiments, separate grenadier regiments, and infantry regiments of superior guard status increased the total. The varied cavalry included cuirassier and dragoon regiments of 10 squadrons each, and lighter hussar and uhlan regiments of 5 each, a squadron being about 150 men. The redoubtable Cossacks and artillery batteries of 4 to 12 pounder guns made a formidable force—officered and commanded by members of the nobility and landed gentry, dedicated to the Czar's service, but not perhaps in the forefront of military methods.

ABOVE, RIGHT: A typical Russian infantryman in a greatcoat and field cap.

BELOW: Russian infantry attack the suburbs of Paris in 1814. They wear the characteristic low Russian shako (kiwer). Those with tall black plumes are grenadiers. Dark green jackets and white trousers formed the basic uniform. They had metal canteens slung on the black knapsacks. The regimental numbers on the cartridge boxes of the nearest men suggest they are light infantry.

Prussia and its Army

IN the north of Central Europe, centuries of struggle, from the days of the Teutonic Knights (between Christian and pagan, German and Slav), had established the large, strong kingdom of Prussia. It had repeated in some ways the growth of Austria, extending its frontiers by treaty, annexation, marriage and unblushing aggression, redeemed somewhat by fostering a regard for progress in agricultural and economic matters, for learning and for internal law and order. The agricultural basis was not too promising, as large areas consisted of marsh, peat moor and sandy heath.

Its position too posed another problem; on a vast open plain, with potential enemies on all sides, it was almost inevitable that to survive at all it had to be militarily strong. Hence authority, discipline, obedience, efficiency, became the watchwords of a centralised bureaucratic state, ruled by the ambitious house of Hohenzollern - Brandenburg from Potsdam and Berlin, in tune with the wishes of a privileged landed nobility, known as Junkers in their large Baltic estates.

Frederick the Great and Frederick II had raised the country to high rank in Europe, though as yet Prussia was unwilling to risk a 'show-down' with Austria over precedence among

Fusilier

At the end of the 17th century when matchlock guns were in general use, special companies of infantry were armed with the more expensive Flintlock musket (or Fusil) and given the job of guarding the Artillery. The matchlock musket needed a smouldering cord (or match) to fire it and sparks from these could cause nasty accidents when they were carried near the large quantities of gunpowder used by the Artillery. The Flintlock needed no match and was therefore much safer. These first soldiers to carry Flintlock 'fusils' became known as fusiliers. Later special regiments of elite troops and in some armies the ordinary line troops were called fusiliers, even though the entire Army was then armed with Flintlocks. A Prussian fusilier of 1807 is shown here.

smaller German states. Their successors, Frederick-William II and III, faced a difficult situation on account of Napoleon, and paid for their indecision with the stinging defeat of Jena in 1806.

The next few years saw a complete overhaul of the humbled state —not in the direction of parliamentary democracy or liberal reform, but rather of administration and military efficiency; and though Prussian troops did form a part of Napoleon's army in Russia, from that time Prussia began to emerge as the chief rival to France on the continent.

Military training brought in fresh troops every six months, so releasing the older men. Each brigade aimed at a balance of all arms—fusiliers, musketeers, grenadiers, with cavalry both heavy (cuirassier or dragoon) and light (uhlan or hussar), and both mounted and unmounted artillery. Infantry strength was increased by detachments of Jägers, largely volunteer riflemen, and after 1813 by Landwehr militiamen. The method of fighting differed from the French one of direct assault by massed grenadiers, as the organisation had no provision for combining brigades in action into larger striking forces.

Rifleman

A rifled gun has a spiral groove cut into the inside of the barrel, which makes the bullet spin and therefore fly straighter—rather like the flights on an arrow. Selected troops were armed with these, traditionally the weapons of huntsmen (Jäger means huntsman in German) and were usually dressed in hunter's dark green coats. They were used as snipers, scouts and skirmishers. The illustration shows a Jäger (rifleman) of the Prussian Garde Jäger battalion in 1809.

GA

Austria and its Army

THE royal house of Hapsburg enjoyed prestige from being for centuries head of the Holy Roman Empire. Its actual territory, known as Austria, was really a polyglot empire of mixed peoples—later termed the 'ramshackle empire'—the chief being German-speaking Austria proper, Magyars in Hungary, groups of north Slavs (like the Czechs of Bohemia and Slovaks of the Carpathians), Poles in Galicia, south Slavs in Croatia and Slovenia, small groups of Germans among the Rumanians of Transylvania, and north Italians.

Although a life of some sophistication was enjoyed by those living in the few large towns—notably Vienna where the arts and music (Haydn, Mozart) were fostered—there was little economic progress, industry and commerce with an attendant middle class being far subordinate to the agricultural basis of the whole vast area. Most people were peasants or even serfs.

Power was exercised by a nobility of large landed families, as in Hungary, and by the German-speaking Austrians who provided leaders and officials. One dominant aspiration shaping policy was the desire to act as 'big brother' to the many small states of southern Germany outside the empire, and another was the need for stability to keep the rickety political structure together—a need that

Cuirassier

The metal breast plate worn by this officer is called a 'cuirass'. Cuirassiers were the last troops to wear armour. Traditionally they were heavy cavalry, mounted on large horses, charging in masses to smash the enemy formations. Only a front plate was worn. The British Army gave up the cuirass in the 18th century. The French Cuirassiers wearing helmet and front and breast plates were well protected. This illustration shows an officer of the Austrian Cuirassier Regiment Hohenzollern-Hechingen, 1812.

was later, at the Congress of Vienna and after, to identify the Austrian representative, Count Metternich, with reaction and repression.

Size and numbers allowed Austria always to be able to put large armies in the field, but their uncertain fortunes must in fact be attributed to the uneven quality of training and the uneven degrees of enthusiasm that the varied groups felt towards Vienna. After failing to cope with Napoleon in north Italy and the Danube valley, the Archduke Charles reorganised the Austrian forces on the lines of the French model of Army Corps, Divisions, Brigades, Regiments and Battalions. In theory, there were 6 companies each, of over 200 fusiliers or ordinary line infantry, per battalion; and each regiment had two grenadier companies of 145 men attached. Deficiencies in time of war were made up from Landwehr battalions of part-time troops, and there were also small detachments of Jägers or riflemen of two companies each. There was artillery (up to 12 lb cannon and 7 lb howitzers), and cavalry in large eight squadron regiments.

BELOW, LEFT TO RIGHT: Austrian grenadier of 1809-1813. Austrian line infantryman of 1809-1815, and Austrian general, 1809.

Watched by Napoleon from the hillside beyond, Bavarian infantry makes an attack against the Austrians.

The South German States

BETWEEN Prussia in the north, Austria to the east, France to the west, and the Alps in the south lies a block of territory watered by Rhine, Main and Danube which is completely German in language and culture, but which in Napoleon's time was just a conglomeration of petty kingdoms, duchies, bishoprics and so on, all nominally independent and separate, but mostly owing some degree of allegiance to the rather vague historical concept of a Holy Roman Emperor. There were several dozen of these miniature states in the political jigsaw, the larger ones including Bavaria (made a kingdom by Napoleon), Baden, Saxony Württemberg and Hesse. Napoleon, on abolishing the Holy Roman Empire, tried to unite the little states in a Confederation of the Rhine, under this presidency. The Congress of Vienna made them into the loose union called the Bund, and it was not until the formation of one united German nation, under Bismarck half a century later, that they were closely bound in one powerful unit.

These lands included many ancient cities, cultural and religious centres, and were the birthplace of many famous figures in art, literature and music. Their military forces, by reason of small size and political separatism, could not amount to a great deal, and in some cases were just groups of mercenaries; but Bavaria and Saxony had armies strong enough to be used by their rulers for political ends.

31

The British Army

THERE were distinct differences from the French. In the first place the army, composed solely of volunteers, reflected the class-structure of society: officers, who bought their commissions, were mainly from the landed gentry, and so were used to riding and to leadership, while 'other ranks' were of humbler origins, and included many who enlisted just for the pay and the cash bonus, or to see the world, or to avoid 'trouble' with the authorities. Results worked out better than might have been expected, and in the century after Marlborough a tradition of discipline and good morale had been established.

The effectiveness and success of the infantry derived from their deployment, their training in 'live' firing, and their good weapons—their musket could be fired four times a minute. A battalion varied from 400 to 1,200 men. Unlike the French it was composed of ten companies, not six; but as with the French the most powerful men would make a more heavily armed, so-called grenadier company, while one company of the smaller but most active men would be the 'light' company who, with a proportion of riflemen,

Light Infantry

Bodies of troops to act as skirmishers and scouts, heading attacks and acting independently from the solid mass of the infantry were necessary and these were usually termed 'light infantry'. In some armies they carried lighter equipment; they usually received special training. The British had light infantry regiments but also every 'Line' infantry regiment had one company of light infantry— usually the smaller, more active men. This drawing shows a private of a British light infantry regiment. The bugle badge was worn by light infantry regiments in the British Army and in some other armies.

32

GAE

acted as skirmishers and sharp-shooters. The remaining eight companies ('line' companies) formed a long line only two ranks deep, trained to stand their ground and fire concerted volleys at the word of command. With the front rank kneeling and the rear rank able to fire over their heads, every musket was in use, and the intensity of fire-power of this 'thin red line' was very great. If confronted by cavalry, a quick manoeuvre could turn the line into a series of squares.

Supporting cavalry regiments were typically composed of four squadrons of up to 200 troopers each, but often lacked adequate campaign experience and were not so famous as their brothers on foot, though well mounted and equipped. Artillery support also was of a high standard as regards guns and men, and gunners were used to doing a fair share of the fighting; but the proportion of guns to infantry was much lower than the French, and they were not integrated so closely under the Commander in Chief, having their own Master General of Ordnance.

A possible weakness in organisation might be suspected here; there was an excellent King's German Legion (reminding one that George III had estates in Hanover), that was 'an army within an army'; and the other army departments (such as the commissariat, supply, quarters and intelligence), were typically under Staff officers or officials who were answerable more to Whitehall than to the Commander in the field.

Napoleon's Italian Campaign 1796-97

This sketch map (which indicates modern frontiers only) shows the sites of principal battles and events, and main geographical features. This campaign is described in Chapter 2, page 9.

4 : Consolidating a
Position, 1798-1803

AUSTRIA was overcome, but England remained. Wisely judging that British sea-power made an invasion premature, Napoleon was attracted by an alternate way of undermining his enemy—a venture into the Mediterranean and Near East, where a 'soft' military success in Egypt could prove a stepping-stone either to further glories against the crumbling Turkish empire or to threatening the British in India. He had long dreamed of a romantic Eastern venture, with himself as a new Alexander; and the idea appealed to many French leaders who thought of the Near East as a natural sphere of French influence, and to others who wanted Napoleon out of the way. To anyone of cool judgment, the whole Egyptian and Syrian Campaign of '98 must appear as a hare-brained escapade, an ill-advised interlude. Yet it is typical of him, and of the way events were

Bonaparte in Egypt. The subjugation of Egypt was not basically an end in itself, but rather a preliminary to further conquests. Having once defeated the Egyptians. Napoleon was at pains to be conciliatory, to show interest in and toleration for their religion and culture, and to adapt to Eastern ways.

The Siege of Acre, 1799. The beginning of the Syrian campaign was marked by French successes, but at Acre the troops were exhausted and plague-ridden. The port was besieged for two months, but with the help of supplies and arms from Sir Sidney Smith managed to hold out, forcing a disappointed Napoleon to change his plans and retire to Egypt instead of continuing through Syria to Constantinople. 'If Acre had fallen I would have changed the face of the world', he claimed. But in view of his limited forces and his difficulties, it seems unlikely that even Napoleon could have succeeded; and it is interesting to speculate that the changed face of the world caused by French success at Acre would not have been the change that Napoleon planned!

running, that even from this apparent failure he was able to derive further credibility, as soldier and political liberator, even as scholar and philosopher.

Leaving in May, with nearly 40,000 troops and an army of scholars and experts, Napoleon forced the surrender of Malta (thus paving the way for a British occupation of the island later), avoided Nelson's squadron, disembarked at Alexandria and inflicted a decisive defeat on the Egyptians at the Pyramids. He then tried by every trick to gain their confidence, posing as liberator and as purveyor of French culture eager

Archeological work being carried out by members of the Institute of Egyptology, watched by soldiers and local natives. Napoleon's expedition initiated popular interest in ancient Egyptian civilisation.

Exit Liberty, the French Way, November 1799. The incident that provoked this satirical cartoon was the appearance at St. Cloud, where the legislative body was meeting, of Napoleon's faithful troops, putting the finishing touches to the coup d'état which established Napoleon's supremacy —albeit after many anxious moments. At the sight of the grenadiers the deputies fled, and the way was open for a new provisional government, the end of Jacobin domination, and the beginning of Napoleon's career as despot—more or less benevolent, according to circumstances!

Bonaparte, First Consul of the French Republic, December 1799. Within a week or two of the coup d'état, Napoleon was formally installed as First Consul, ie, head of state. It has been well said that if 'Liberty, Equality, Fraternity' had dimmed, a new motto of 'splendour, comprehension and efficiency' had arisen.

to understand the Mohammedan world. (Archeology did benefit from the expedition: the Rosetta stone was found and the deciphering of ancient Egyptian history began.)

Nelson's victory in August at Aboukir Bay marooned Napoleon in the Nile valley, but he was saved from embarrassment by a threat from Turkey and Syria which gave him the excuse to move north-east. French arms under his leadership, in spite of thirst and disease from the unaccustomed desert, again carried all before them until held up at the port of Acre, besieged from March to May 1799, and able to hold out with the help of a British squadron under Sir Sidney Smith. Again Napoleon appeared to be out on a limb, but a Turkish landing at the Nile delta provided a challenge that he accepted with typical speed and resolution: forced marches brought his faithful troops back to Cairo by mid-June, and in spite of casualties and disease, shortage of food and of ammunition, he all but annihilated the Turkish invaders at Aboukir on July 25. A month later he left secretly for France, leaving his troops under General Kléber. To many this might seem sheer selfish desertion, but news had reached him of a new threat to the republic at home, of a re-alliance of the autocratic powers, of new trouble in Italy, and of in-competence in Paris, where the Directory of five now represented supreme power, as the Republic had no personal president. Here was a chance for a patriot and a strong man to help his country, especially when driven by personal ambition and a belief in his 'destiny'.

The 'dangerous corners' that he had skidded round in his Near Eastern venture were forgotten; that it had all come to naught was of no matter against the lustre of a romantic adventure—not at least in the minds and hearts of an anxious and perplexed nation. Napoleon was back by October to a rapturous welcome; and profiting from this public mood, and from the lack of confidence in the inept national leaders in Assembly and Directory, he proceeded to make himself master of France.

He used every trick imaginable. He would have had little to learn even from 20th century politicians in the art of projecting an acceptable 'public image' as soldier, statesman, scholar: speeches, intrigues, the latent threat of his personally loyal troops encamped just outside Paris, the help of one of the Directory itself (Abbé Siéyès), the rigging of com-mittees, all culminated in a melodramatic coup d'état in November, which ended the long succession of Jacobin-dominated assemblies and councils which had ruled France for ten years, and revised the constitution, making Napoleon head of state as First Consul, with power to choose ministers and decide policy. There were two other consuls, but, like the other new organs of state, they were largely a facade. It is hard to say how far the French were deceived, but his personal prestige and his wisdom (or cunning?) in doing nothing positive to upset the land settlement, and the republican ideal followed since 1789 made it all acceptable to the great mass of the French people.

Thus by the first days of the new century the stage was set for a complete re-organisation of France; but further diplomatic and military

RIGHT: Murat, King of Naples. Born March 25, 1767 near Cahors, he gained rapid promotion in the Revolutionary army and identified himself with Napoleon, serving as a brilliant commander of cavalry in the first Italian campaign, in Egypt and at Marengo. Became Marshal, and married Caroline, Napoleon's youngest sister, and reaped further high honours and financial rewards when the Empire was established. Distinguished service at Austerlitz, Jena and Eylau was followed by his proclamation as King of Naples. At the time of the Russian expedition he became critical of Napoleon. Though he was trusted and left in command of the retreating army, and fought with distinction at Dresden and Leipzig, he was increasingly guided by personal considerations and tried for a time to make a deal with the allies. Turning again to support Napoleon in the Hundred Days, he acted impetuously and against orders in trying to make himself King of all Italy, was thwarted in this by the Austrians, and incurred the Emperor's wrath. He did not appear at Waterloo. At Napoleon's final overthrow, he fled to Corsica and thence to Calabria in the south of his former kingdom, posing as liberator; but he was imprisoned and met death by the firing-squad on October 13, 1815.

adventures had to be made immediately. The new Continental Coalition, with Austria again in the lead, was threatening France in the Low Countries, along the Rhine, and had won back northern Italy. In view of the quality of generals like Moreau and Masséna, a victory for French arms was quite likely in any case; but with Napoleon himself keen on smashing Austrian aims again, an exciting second Italian campaign quickly developed. A dramatic crossing of the Alps in May 1800, via Swiss territory and the St Bernard Pass, brought Napoleon to Milan,

The Plum-Pudding in Danger, 1803. When the Treaty of Amiens, 1802, was seen to be only a breathing-space and not a real peace settlement, there was much antagonistic and satirical comment, especially by Britain, against the ambitions of the French dictator: 'The globe itself is too small to satisfy such insatiable appetites'. Napoleon was always very sensitive to cartoons and caricatures, and had even attempted at Amiens to extract a promise from the British government that they should be banned!

cutting off the Austrians under Melas, who had forced the capitulation of Genoa on the coast. The resultant battle of Marengo in June, a near thing for Napoleon who practically lost the battle in the morning but won it back in the afternoon with heavy casualties, was not enough to bring Austria to the peace negotiations until the French Army of the Rhine, under Moreau, had pushed into Bavaria and gained a famous victory at Hohenlinden in December. The Peace of Lunéville restored the Campo-Formio situation and confirmed French ascendancy in Europe.

Napoleon tried to exploit this by building, early in 1801, a (short-lived) coalition of his own to isolate Britain; but victories by British fleets in the Mediterranean and at Copenhagen (under Nelson) persuaded him to reach a peace with Britain in order to gain time for naval improvement—the Treaty of Amiens, early in 1802. This delay must have been galling to Napoleon, whose restless nature demanded constant action and advance. It mattered little to him that Britain made many concessions, giving up newly won colonial gains in the West Indies and the Cape, and agreeing to evacuate Malta, while French armies remained strongly entrenched over all western Europe. His realisation that Britain was his greatest opponent, that his ambitions could never be achieved while the

A famous political cartoon by Gillray, dated 1803, which depicts Napoleon — 'Boney' to the English—threatening England. The Roast Beef of Old England (between the defender's feet) symbolises the danger to the British way of life.

Plans for attacking England, 1804. This contemporary engraving was intended to show the lengths to which Napoleon's imagination went in his desire to stage a cross-channel invasion of Britain—doubly interesting perhaps in the light of more modern developments. Balloons, troopships, and a channel tunnel are all depicted.

'nation of shipkeepers'—a sarcastic reference to British trade—remained undefeated, made him continue his war preparations. He did nothing to allay Britain's suspicions, and was too impatient to await the re-building of a large fleet before planning his further ventures—or even starting them, like the ill-advised and largely unnecessary expedition to re-establish French power against Toussaint l'Ouverture, the negro leader of San Domingo. The uneasy and unreal 'peace' was broken by the reluctance of Britain to withdraw her troops from Malta, in the face of French designs in the Mediterranean.

So once again France was put on a war footing, and Napoleon carried the nation with him, with what today would be called 'hand-outs' to the Press, and a fighting speech to the Senate in May 1803. Success in so many things but not in the main objective—his power had been increased in 1802 when he was made Consul for life—was trying his patience and impairing his judgment, and an occasional outburst revealed that he realised his own position at home; but, like most self-made despots and autocrats, he found that, once started, he had to go on.

5: The Empire— Success and Exploitation, 1804-1808

NAPOLEON had brought France to leadership on the continent, and it was going to look the part: he was nothing if not thorough! A start at bringing France into her rightful place in diplomatic and social circles, at showing the world that France had 'arrived', had already been made. Nor was it just a matter, in modern jargon, of 'keeping up with the Jones's'. Napoleon was concerned with the best and the successful, in every sphere: Paris was to be the cultural centre of Europe, and in re-designing the city with stately boulevards and fine public buildings, he called on architects and engineers, administrators and scholars, without regard to birth or previous allegiance so long as they were willing to work hard in his present service. He, who said of his army that every common soldier carried a field marshal's baton in his knapsack, offered a 'career open to talent', and himself set the example.

He worked to establish a strongly centralised system of government: it spelled efficiency, it suited France, and it suited his own wishes as benevolent despot. Social privilege, enshrined under the 'ancien régime' and abolished by the revolution, was rigidly suppressed, and security for the vast new class of small peasant proprietors was confirmed and their place in the economic life of France remains to this day. The new decoration for public services, the Legion of Honour, was of course non-hereditary. To cool religious passions and enlist further support, a new accommodation with the Catholic Church had been arrived at in the Concordat of August 1802; it lasted a century. (The Church had to acquiesce in the loss of lands and revenue, and could no longer be 'a State within a State', but it was re-established and recognised as the official religion of France, and individuals were free to follow it or not as they chose.) Perhaps most important of all, the preparatory work of simplifying and improving the legal system was brought to fruition in 1804 by the adoption of the Civil Code, a handbook, as it were, setting out the principles of justice and equity in a tolerant, democratic society. Napoleon laid no claim to being a lawyer, but his incisive mind had much influence on the clarity of the final document and the speed of its compilation.

The prosperity that was coming to France, and the restoration of lustre

Execution of the Duc d'Enghien, March 1804. The abduction of this young member of the former royal family, his summary 'trial' and immediate execution in the moat at Vincennes (though the charge of complicity in a plot was known to be groundless) shows the ruthless side of the policy on which Napoleon had embarked in his desire to be undisputed master.

to a tarnished public life, were sullied, it is true, by some ruthless and tyrannical acts. Royalist sentiment in Vendée in the far west had been behind an attempted assassination of Napoleon and a coup to overthrow him; treachery and arbitrary arrests, of which Napoleon must have known, disposed of the leaders, while the situation was exploited to discredit and deport other political malcontents at the Jacobin end of the political scale. Further, when in 1804, the Duc d'Enghien, a young prince of the old royal house of Bourbon, was kidnapped, summarily tried and shot without any real evidence of conspiracy, Napoleon was party to a crime that he must have often later regretted.

Still Napoleon was not satisfied. Here at the start of this period in 1804, one almost has the feeling that in spite of being Consul for life, and more powerful than ever, he was in fact being propelled by events and circumstances, rather than himself directing them. There is a certain inevitability about the course of events that reminds one that no man, however influential, can be entirely free from the results of his own actions. Violence is apt to breed counter violence; and whether it was the existence of conspiracies, or whether it was by his own ruthless policy in dealing with them, Napoleon certainly became irritable and suspicious, and anxious to safeguard his own position; public opinion, especially in the middle classes, peasantry and army, wished to avoid the possible chaos and anarchy of a further revolution. People saw that Napoleon was indentified with stability and order, as well as military glory and national prestige. Thus, with Moreau conveniently banished for alleged royalist sympathies, and with Napoleon himself dissatisfied even with a life consulate, it came as no surprise when France was proclaimed an hereditary empire in 1804. A compliant Senate in May voted him 'Emperor of the French', a public plebiscite confirmed this, the succession (should Josephine continue childless) was settled on

43

NAPOLEON

Engraved by William Holl.

NAPOLEON I.

44

A contemporary print depicting in fanciful fashion the French Army embarking in troopships for the proposed invasion of Britain. The group on the right portrays Napoleon and his staff observing proceedings.

Napoleon's brothers Joseph and Louis and he took the imperial crown from the Pope's hands in December. Napoleon had himself arranged the coronation ceremony, and in crowning himself he was asserting that his imperial dignity had been made by the nation and the army, and not by the Church.

The establishment of a new royal court in Europe gave an opportunity for pomp and circumstance on a grand scale. Napoleon himself had no time for etiquette and the social graces; but he appreciated the appeal of royalty and pageantry to the public, it was now easy to turn any state occasion into a great public show ('bread and circuses') and the whole world could see that just as France had 'arrived', so had the Bonapartes! Napoleon now began the process of finding lucrative posts for his family, treating them on much the same lines as all his other appointments, viz rewards and encouragement for acknowledging him as head of the family. Nor was this altogether a case of 'jobs for the boys': his brothers in general were men of parts, and his regard for his mother Letizia was deep and genuine. A new élite also was created, a new 'aristocracy of merit' to give distinction to the court; but though the titles were high-sounding and the uniforms and helmets glittering, it was all rather synthetic and self-conscious, and must have prompted many a discreet smile by those who could remember the 'ancien régime'. (Their discretion would also have prompted them to keep quiet!)

In all this period, 1803-1805, his personal aggrandisement and the satisfaction of outward show never removed from Napoleon's mind his dominating desire to humble England. He made preparations for invasion by training a vast band of conscripts to swell 'la Grande Armée' to over 200,00 men stationed along the Channel coast. Huge sums were spent on improving the roads in northern France and in the feverish building of a giant fleet of flat-bottomed transports. British naval vigilance, however, in the shape of Nelson hovering off Toulon and

Mail coach brings news of defeat at Trafalgar, 1805. The day after Napoleon's capture of Ulm in the Danube valley, emphasising French power on the continent, came the decisive naval victory of Nelson off Cape Trafalgar in the south of Spain on October 21, 1805, confirming British command of the sea and liberating Britain from the fear of invasion. The means of communication were relatively primitive, and news could not be 'flashed' from point to point: mail coaches with fixed time-schedules, (replacing the earlier system of mounted post-boys). were only just coming into their own: the improved Palmer's mail-coach had only started in England in 1784. Better roads, in Britain and on the continent, gave the coach its chance, though its ascendancy was relatively short-lived, as railways came in with the 1830s.

Cornwallis off Brittany frustrated the assembly of a French fleet large enough to cover a Channel crossing, in spite of clever ruses to send British squadrons off on wild goose chases. British sea-power proved the ultimate deterrent, and Napoleon gave up the idea of direct assault in August 1805, a few weeks before Nelson's great victory at Trafalgar against Villeneuve's combined French and Spanish fleet finally clinched the matter.

Napoleon later claimed (with little credibility) that the whole project had been a giant bluff, and that his preparations were really for a renewal of hostilities on the continent. He certainly brought this about with his customary speed and confidence: a series of calculated provocations, (notably his assumption of kingship over the republic of Lombardy, the former Austrian territory in Italy). goaded the Hapsburg rulers of much-humiliated Austria into mobilising and joining with Britain (now under Prime Minister Pitt) and Russia in a new coalition. Napoleon switched his army at lightning speed across Germany, and cut off the unprepared Austrian general Mack at Ulm on the Danube. He pressed on towards Vienna, and appeared to be himself caught in a trap in Moravia, as, in addition to the remaining Austrian armies and their Russian allies, a huge Prussian army was now to his rear. (Prussia had been provoked by the passage of French troops across her territory and her ruler Frederick William III had made an alliance with the Czar). Quite un-deterred, Napoleon's seasoned troops under commanders like Soult and Murat gained a resounding victory against a combined Russian and

46

The Eve of Austerlitz, December 1805. Napoleon's confidence was increased when, before dawn, he went with Marshal Soult to visit the bivouacs. His troops lit straw torches to light the way, and welcomed him with cries of 'Long live the Emperor'.

Austrian army at Austerlitz on December 2, 1805. The battle went according to Napoleon's plan and time-table, underlining once more his prowess as a military commander. Before the end of the month the Treaty of Schönbrunn gave him ascendancy among the small states of southern Germany, and also in Italy where the Hapsburgs had ruled in the Kingdom of Naples in the south.

His position seemed impregnable: 'Roll up that map', Pitt is said to have stated after Austerlitz, as it must have seemed that the old map

The day before the Battle of Austerlitz. Napoleon was calm and completely confident before the great battle of Austerlitz. He believed in the 'personal touch', argued and joked with his soldiers, and slept in a hut behind the front. This print is from a Raffet drawing. Note the Imperial Guard sentry in attendance.

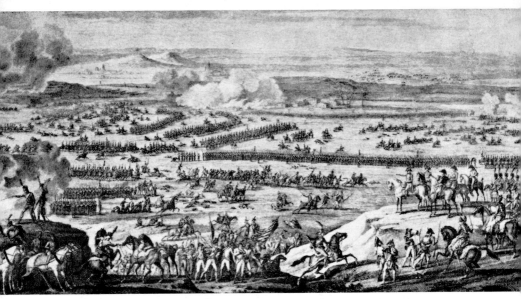

Battle of Austerlitz, December 2, 1805. The style of fighting, the hand to hand encounters, the close formations, were almost bound to give rise to grievous casualties. In this famous French victory the combined Russian and Austrian army of about 90,000 men suffered 23,000 dead and wounded, and 20,000 prisoners. Napoleon himself spent nearly the whole night locating the French wounded, who were numerous 'Never was a battlefield so horrible . . . . one's heart bled', he reported. Yet, decisive as the battle seemed, it was to be nearly another ten years before Europe was free from bloodshed. ABOVE: A famous Vernet print showing the battlefield, Napoleon and staff to the right. BELOW: Line infantry making an attack. Note the drummers repeating commands by drum—probably the 'advance' in this case. This is from a Raffet print.

Napoleon directing the deployment of columns, Battle of Jena, October 1806. This battle, which did so much to humiliate Prussia, was another of the many famous occasions when Napoleon was right in the front line, among his troops. He boasted, in a letter to Josephine, of how fit he was—'I am extremely well . . . I have put on weight . . . I get up at midnight'. He was certainly up and about the night before Jena, choosing his ground (a small plateau dominating the countryside), finding rough paths to bring up the cannon, even holding the lanterns while his men manhandled the guns into position, and then probing his own forward positions (and nearly getting shot by one of his sentries for his pains!). When the battle was joined he directed his men into formation, telling them that their courage would destroy the Prussian cavalry, just as they had crushed the Russian infantry at Austerlitz. And so it worked out. Note the Chasseurs à Cheval of the Guard at left in this Raffet engraving.

of European frontiers had been made permanently out-of-date by Napoleon's successes.

The south German states, notably Bavaria, Baden and Würrtemberg, freed from Austrian leadership, were completely in Napoleon's camp, their ruling houses united in marriage with members of the Bonaparte family. The old Holy Roman Empire, headed by the Hapsburgs of Austria, was abolished in June 1806, and its place taken by a Confederation of the Rhine, with Napoleon at its head. Yet he was aware of a gap: he had got to have the co-operation of the whole continent if he was to undermine Britain by closing European ports to British ships,—his new ambitious plan now that invasion was 'off'. So King Frederick William of Prussia was provoked into mobilising his army, which, poorly led, was completely out-manoeuvred and suffered crushing defeats at Jena, from Napoleon and at Auerstadt, from Marshal Davout. This stunning blow was in October 1806 and was followed up so vigorously that by November Napoleon was in the Prussian capital, Berlin, issuing the

Napoleon directs artillery assault at Battle of Eylau, in February, 1807. Napoleon had intended to keep to winter quarters and resume his struggle against Russians and Prussians when the weather improved. The Russian commander Bennigsen, however, threatened him from the direction of the Baltic coast, so Napoleon resumed the offensive, hoping for a conclusive victory. The battle of Eylau was fought under terrible conditions of frozen slush and blinding snow. It was costly to both sides, as heavy artillery bombardments were a dominant feature; in fact at one point Napoleon himself used the ramrod and trained the cannon. But in spite of losing half his men killed, Bennigsen managed to retreat in order, and claimed he was not defeated.

famous decrees (later known as the Continental System), which prohibited all trade with Britain from either North Sea or Baltic ports.

The final touches were added by a further advance through what had been Poland, to deal with a surviving remnant of the Prussian army, which with Russian support was on the borders of East Prussia. A costly and inconclusive battle at Prussisch-Eylau was followed by errors in manoeuvring by the Russian commanders which Napoleon was quick to exploit in a resounding victory at Friedland. The young Czar Alexander, imagining himself in danger, came quickly to a conference with Napoleon, held on a raft in the River Niemen, and by the Peace of Tilsit, July 1807, made an alliance with him, secretly agreeing to join the Continental System to ruin British commerce.

It can be said that this marked the zenith of Napoleon's career, militarily, diplomatically, territorially, in every way. With the hind-sight of today, however, we can see that the first faint signs that there would be an end to the road were about to appear.

OPPOSITE: Sketch map shows principal battles, cities and locations of Napoleon's campaigns in Central Europe, 1805-1813. Scale of map: 1 inch=85 miles.

Napoleon meets Czar Alexander, June 1807. After the French victory at Friedland the Russian Army was pursued to the river Niemen, and an armistice was then signed. Three days later Emperor and Czar met at Tilsit, on a raft in mid-river, for peace discussions. It could have proved a difficult meeting, but Napoleon really needed the co-operation of Russia in his designs to ruin British trade, so was moved to be reasonable and make concessions.

6: Cracks in the Edifice, 1808-1812

THE days of glory were far from over, of course. Although the Empire could now be indentified with tasteless, elaborate furniture and extremes of dress (frills and fringes, tight pantaloons and absurdly high collars), as much as with pomp and dignity, further advances in the life of France were made, with more or less lasting effect, notably the state-controlled University of France established in 1808. Further military success came

Battle of Wagram, July 1809. Mounted on his white charger, Euphrates, (a gift from the Shah of Persia), Napoleon views the field of battle in typical fashion. The outcome was of vital importance to him, as a recent set-back in crossing the Danube had raised the hopes of European nations eager for his defeat. It proved a victory against the Austrians under the Archduke Charles, but a hard-won success.

Napoleon wounded at Ratisbon, April 1809. Napoleon was not in the habit of doing his staff work behind the lines; he had the whole terrain in his mind before a battle began, and preferred to be mounted and in close touch with the fighting and his field commanders. In driving the Austrians from Ratisbon, en route for Vienna, he received a slight wound in the ankle. His surgeon Yvan cut away the boot, dressed the wound, and Napoleon at once re-mounted to ride along the front, re-assuring the troops and boosting morale.

in 1809, when Austria, so often humiliated, and now indignant over Napoleon's treatment of the Royal house of Spain, tried to rally the south German states to free Germany and cut down the despot's power. With his usual vicious rapidity, Napoleon forced the Austrian army back from Bavaria along the Danube. When he appeared to be in danger from the scattering of his forces, he re-grouped, forced the Austrians to abandon Ratisbon, and moved towards Vienna. Here, in crossing the great river, he met with serious losses and reverses, destroying the myth of his invincibility, and it was only with a reinforced army that he just managed to win the battle of Wagram. The 'bright sun of Austerlitz' had dimmed, but, in the unofficial truce that followed, events in other areas turned out favourably for France and ill for Austria. So in the peace that was signed at Vienna in October 1809 fresh

Defeat of French at Baylen, July 1808. In Andalusia in the south, small patriotic Spanish armies were better organised than elsewhere. The one under General Castaños succeeded in forcing the surrender of General Dupont's troops, who had sacked Cordoba, at Baylen. This victory fired the enthusiasm of Spaniards everywhere, showing that the French were not invincible. In this Raffet engraving Spanish troops examine the gear of disarmed prisoners.

humiliations were heaped on Austria and more territorial losses along the Adriatic, and within a few months, Napoleon, ever a fast mover, had had his marriage to (childless) Josephine dissolved, and had gained the hand of the Austrian Archduchess Maria-Louisa, so effecting a Franco-Austrian alliance, of sorts!

However, the writing was on the wall for all to see, albeit faintly. The French people themselves, now that fair stability and prosperity had been achieved within enlarged frontiers, were ready to cry 'Enough' to further adventures; the peoples of Central Europe, bearing much of the financial burden of Napoleon's ambitions, and worried by conscription, billeting and reparations, were ill-disposed toward him. In Spain, which he tried to dragoon into joining his continental embargo on British trade, he found himself up against an obstinate popular movement: the Spanish people had little to thank their Bourbon rulers for, but when in 1808 Charles IV was deposed and replaced by Napoleon's brother Joseph, their patriotic feelings were aroused just at the time when they, as devout Catholics, were strongly incensed over Napoleon's high-handed incorporation of Rome into the French Empire, and were still smarting from the way they had been coerced into supporting France at the time of Trafalgar. Napoleon's interference in Spain was prompted partly by his wish to subdue Portugal, Britain's

Napoleon's second marriage, March 1810. A union with one of Europe's oldest royal houses, the Hapsburgs, was bound to appeal to a man of Napoleon's ambition. (He had always been impressed, too, by the apparent popularity of the Hapsburgs, in spite of the defeats and humiliations he had heaped on them). The young Austrian Archduchess Maria-Louisa only eighteen, was at first averse to the suggestion, though this was kept from Napoleon, whose eagerness prompted him to defy both convention and the pouring rain by going forward to meet her on her way to Compiègne, actually intercepting her carriage in the village of Courcelles, as depicted in this engraving.

Napoleon and staff ride to meet the King of Naples, June 1808. Napoleon forced the abdication of the Spanish King Charles IV, and placed his own brother Joseph on the Spanish throne. Joseph had been King of Naples since 1806, and his place was taken by Murat, one of Napoleon's most ambitious marshals, who had married Napoleon's sister Caroline. These 'arrangements', the shuffling around of kingships as if they were stages in promotion, were mostly conducted at Bayonne in south-west France. Joseph's elevation was to prove anything but peaceful!

Napoleon rejects appeal of citizens of Madrid. Encouraged by their victory over the French at Baylen, by the early British successes in Portugal and the food and equipment from Britain that was reaching their guerillas, and imbued with intense nationalist feeling against the French invader and the foreign king (Napoleon's brother Joseph), the Spaniards posed a real threat to the Emperor in late 1808. He went himself to Spain, with a huge army under some of his best commanders, and forced his way to Madrid. He received the submission of the inhabitants December 1808, haughtily telling them to accept Joseph and the laws of Napoleon.

oldest ally, and force it more completely into the Continental System; but though his political schemes and intrigues appear cunningly designed, his whole treatment of the Spanish situation was really a blunder —another sign that he was no longer the man he was.

In any case, the Continental System was by no means a complete success. As so often happens with blockades, embargoes, sanctions and such like, there were loopholes and much smuggling. Britain had struck back with Orders in Council which amounted to blockading Europe in respect of a whole range of essential materials and food, and the Royal Navy upheld its right to stop and search vessels bound for European ports. It is true that here and there the effect could be side-stepped, as it were, eg, by growing the hitherto unpopular potato for food, by growing chicory as coffee substitute, or by experimenting with sugar-extraction from beet, since imported cane was not available;

but the 'squeeze' by British sea-power was real enough to make many European peoples resentful of Napoleon's policies. As far as the continental meal table and wardrobe were concerned it was a reality, though it is interesting to learn that some of the high-class cloth for French officers' uniforms was produced in Lancashire and Yorkshire! (Legal prohibitions may be made, but where goods of high quality and desirability are concerned there are always smugglers and 'black market' dealers willing to take a chance, and public officials who will 'turn a blind eye', for a consideration!)

It was the situation in Spain and Portugal however that did more than anything else to start a slide in Napoleon's fortunes. Large armies, totalling 300,000 of his best troops under five or six of his most experienced marshals, were pinned down in the peninsula in an attempt to contain the Spanish rising inflamed by nationalist and religious feeling. Some at least of the official Spanish army had to be reckoned with (other units having been drafted to northern Europe); there were guerrilla bands operating locally with fair success, and after August

Napoleon and Staff cross the Guadarrama mountains in late December, 1808. The threat from Sir John Moore's expeditionary force in Old Castile made Napoleon turn north-west and re-cross the Guadarramas in appalling winter conditions. Moore, fearing to be caught between forces under Ney and Soult, decided to retreat and was pursued towards Corunna; but bad news from France obliged Napoleon to return post-haste on January 17, 1809, leaving his marshals in charge. They pressed on, but were too slow to prevent the embarkation of the British forces.

Portuguese Auxiliaries, March 1811. From time to time in the course of the Peninsular War, a 'scorched earth' policy was ordered to make it difficult for the French to live off the country. The Portuguese volunteers of 1809 had been trained as proper auxiliary units by 1810, proving good soldiers, and are here seen dealing ruthlessly with peasants who had not destroyed their homes and food supplies, and were therefore suspected of being 'collaborators' with the French.

1808 there was the expeditionary force of British troops that, aided by command of the sea, had established a 'second front' against Napoleon based on a small beach-head on the Portuguese coast north of Lisbon. This landing began the Peninsular War, which ultimately took British troops across the peninsula into France itself six years later in 1814, becoming one of the greatest sustained military efforts of all time. It was costly to France in manpower and money, but above all it brought to the front Sir Arthur Wellesley (later Duke of Wellington), one of the greatest commanders ever, and in the opinion of some military historians the only undefeated first-rank general in history.

Operations began modestly, as the army numbered only 15,000 (until the Portuguese, who were to prove good soldiers, were adequately trained), and there were deficiencies in transport animals, wagons and cavalry. The two first victories, at Rolica against Delaborde and at Vimiero against Junot, showed Wellesley's abilities to the full: an eye for the country, skilful deployment of units, in and out of the battle line, and the use of skirmishers—a concept developed by Sir John Moore from study of the French infantry tactics. All this secured the liberation of Portugal. Wellesley's temporary departure left Sir John Moore in command. A spirit of over-optimism, occasioned by a Spanish defeat of a French army at Baylen in the south and the abandonment of Madrid, was quenched by the arrival in Spain of Napoleon himself with a huge new army. Under pressure from Marshal Soult in the north and Marshal Ney further south, Moore retired towards Corunna, where the army embarked, under constant attack from the French, having at least drawn the enemy away from southern Spain. It was here at the battle of Corunna that General Sir John Moore was killed.

Wellesley was back in Portugal in the spring of 1809, and at once started clearing the French from the north, which they had re-occupied. (Battle of Oporto). Moving east into Spain, he joined forces with the Spanish and marched to Talavera on the Tagus where he again inflicted a defeat on the French. Lack of numbers prevented a proper follow-up, and this, coupled with the danger of lengthening lines of communication,

Birth of Napoleon's son, March 1811. The birth of a son seemed to Napoleon to set a seal on his success, ensuring an heir and confirming the future of the Empire. The baby, given the title of King of Rome, (evocative of past imperial glory), was presented significantly enough to Napoleon's military intimates as well as to diplomatic dignitaries, and was baptised in Notre Dame on June 9, 1811, at one of the most magnificent ceremonies of all time.

prompted a withdrawal to Portugal. The famous defensive fortifications, the lines of Torres Vedras north of Lisbon, were improved, and a further incursion by the French under Masséna, Ney and Junot was soundly repulsed by Wellesley, now Duke of Wellington, at Busaco in September 1810. The next year was spent in capturing French strong-points and garrisons along the Spanish-Portuguese frontier (Fuentes, Albuera, Ciudad Rodrigo and Badajoz), so that another eastward advance across Spain became possible, culminating in a victory at Salamanca against Marshal Marmont in July 1812. This time the victory was exploited, temporarily at least, by further advances to Valladolid, Madrid and even Burgos in October, but again numerical inferiority prompted a withdrawal, followed in 1813 by Wellington's final offensive, via Vitoria, San Sebastian and the western Pyrenees into France itself early in 1814.

The campaign had been a tough and long drawn-out affair much marked by back-pedalling due to limited resources and political bickering. However, Wellington had proved himself a master strategist and tactician, never giving battle except on ground of his own choosing. New tactics by the British infantryman had brought results and challenged one of Napoleon's favourite formulae—that of massed attacks in columns supported by artillery and cavalry. To the ordinary foot-soldier it was a peculiarly cruel campaign. No soldier past or present has had other than discomfort, dirt, disease, danger and death as his constant companions, but the Peninsular War was exceptionally brutal.

In the first place, the terrain in the peninsula, especially the vast, arid, grim plateau that makes up much of the interior, is a problem in itself: bare rocky ridges, rivers in steep-sided trench-like valleys, thirsty uplands with few fertile areas for extra food; summer months that are African in their grilling temperatures, glaring sun and dusty winds, pitiless to a man in red serge tunic and full pack; winters whose icy winds and driving sleet make even a greatcoat no better than paper. Add to these privations the state of the roads—none of them paved, just beaten tracks of hard earth, rocks and shaly rubble, rutted, pitted and pot-holed to such an extent that wagons had often to be man-handled over most of their journeys. Add to this the general conditions of supply, hygiene, etc, of that period: no motorised units or troop-carriers, no mobile field kitchens, no convenient helicopters to lift reinforcements in or wounded out, no ambulances and Red Cross, just the bumping ox-cart for the wounded, en route to amputation by an over-worked surgeon knowing little or nothing of antiseptic surgery and having no pain-killing drugs. For those who escaped injury there was a pannikin of dirty water, a ration of often doubtful meat and bread, and a blanket beside the fire (as tents only arrived late in the campaign) with snake or scorpion for company! For the French it was worse: they had the added danger of the guerrilla fighters with their various tortures and 'unfriendly natives' to reckon with. Certainly a cruel campaign but by the standards of the day it was pretty luxurious compared with the conditions prevailing in some parts of Britain at the time.

At least the troops could be sure of a meal at some time and clothes on their backs while the civilian was in danger of starving to death on the meagre wages paid for long hard hours in factories, mines and on the farms. In many cases the men had joined up because of this, or alter-

The Duke of Wellington. The Hon Arthur Wellesley came from an Anglo-Irish family, and was probably born in Dublin on April 29, 1769. After Eton he attended a French military school at Angers, but in youth showed few signs of distinction. He began his military service in 1787 as ensign in a foot regiment. Family influence gained him rapid promotion and he entered parliament; but his resourcefulness on a minor military mission in the Low Countries, followed by sound service as soldier and administrator in India from 1797 to 1805, made him a good choice for leading the expeditionary force to Portugal in 1808 and for the long-drawn out Peninsular War, in which he showed all the qualities of a great commander, particularly of infantry. His victory at Waterloo ended his active service, and from then until his death in 1852 he devoted himself to political life.

natively they had been imprisoned for stealing food, not in large quantities but usually for something as small as a loaf of bread. With harsh laws like this that could imprison, hang or deport men for such petty offences, the prisons soon became overcrowded. In order to clear these prisons a periodical clearance was made, the prisoners being given the choice of being shipped out to the penal colonies in Australia (where something like fifty per cent of the prisoners died either en route or

ABOVE: Marshal Ney. Born at Saarlouis, January 10, 1769, the same year as Napoleon and Wellington, he began his military career as a non-commissioned hussar officer when the revolution came, fighting in the Rhine Valley adjoining his home region. His dash and daring quickly earned promotion in the Army of the Rhine. He became Marshal of France, perhaps the most celebrated of Napoleon's generals, when the Empire was formed; and though a disagreement with Masséna (then his superior) kept him out of much of the Peninsular War, he was identified with almost every other campaign—in the Danube valley, at Jena, Eylau, Smolensk, Borodino—while in the retreat from Moscow his gallant rear-guard actions saved the army from complete annihilation. His almost reckless courage earned him the description of 'le brave des braves' from Napoleon; on the day of Waterloo he had five horses shot from under him! Having accepted the restored Louis XVIII at the time of Elba, his support for his old master in the Hundred Days made him technically a traitor, and he was condemned and shot on December 7, 1815—a cruel end for one of the finest soldiers of all time.

from overwork when they got there), joining the army, in which case they got back some of their self-respect and were even paid occasionally, or being press-ganged into the navy. Of the three alternatives it is not surprising that many men chose the army as their 'new start in life'.

However it would be untrue to say that the majority of the British Army was made up from this sweeping of the jails. A great many of the men in fact came from the local militia units that were raised and trained throughout Britain as a form of 'National Guard' and as such were recruited from a good class of men who helped to form the backbone of the British Army. For them therefore the campaign must have been a lot harder than for the 'jail-birds' as they had more to lose. However this does not seem to have put them off and in the fashion of soldiers the world over they made the best of things and in some cases returned to Britain better off than when they left it.

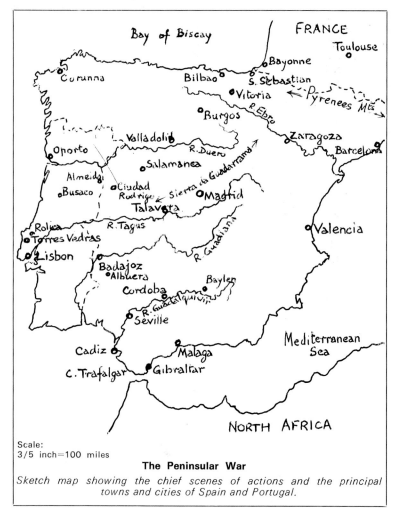

Scale:
3/5 inch=100 miles

The Peninsular War

Sketch map showing the chief scenes of actions and the principal towns and cities of Spain and Portugal.

7: Downfall—Nemesis by Degrees, 1812-1815

NAPOLEON refused to read the signs, attempted to direct operations in Spain by 'remote control', under-rated the difficulties in Spanish geography, and entered what was to be the final struggle with his usual confidence. In an age when rulers were not compelled to act with one eye on a watchful public press, when communication of every type was slow—no railways, or telephones, or wireless telegraphy—Napoleon stuck quite naturally to the energetic enforcement of his despotic powers, completely under-rating the spirit of national patriotism in Britain, Spain, Russia and Prussia which his own actions had inflamed: the quick swoop by security police, the firing squad, the 'whiff of grape-shot' are of limited use against a truly nation-wide mass movement. Despots, even benevolent ones, become blinded by their own attitudes: 'all power corrupts, and absolute power corrupts absolutely'.

Obsessed by the wealth of British trade, he failed to see that it was British industry and manufacture that really underlay British strength. The careful stewardship of Prime Minister Walpole in the first half of the 18th century, the lucky circumstance of coal and iron being found in abundance and near tide-water, had given Britain an early start in the change to mass-production in manufacture; by the period 1800 to 1810 she was already known as 'the workshop of the world' through her vast output of cloth and engineering products, and having successfully harnessed the power of steam for her factory machines since 1785, was standing on the verge of a great break-through in its extended use for locomotion, by sea or land. The social cost of the new methods and organisation was great, but it was to some extent the more readily borne as it kept ships and armies equipped and provided subsidies for allies on the continent.

Napoleon's obstinate determination to undermine British trade and prosperity by his Continental System caused him to make his second great blunder—at the eastern end of Europe this time, just as the first had been in Spain and Portugal in the west. Sensing a 'cooling off' on the part of Czar Alexander, in spite of the accord at Tilsit and a further meeting at Erfurt, he asked for further co-operation in the control of imports. This was refused, as Russia had to get tropical goods from somewhere, and in any case was smarting over Napoleon's re-creation of the Grand Duchy of Warsaw, the possible nucleus of a revived Poland.

Poles meet Napoleon at Vilna. Poland, one of the great states of medieval Europe, had been broken up in 1797 and, losing its national independence, had had its territory divided between Russia, Austria and Prussia. Before the opening of the Russian campaign, when everything was in the balance, Napoleon felt he had to decide against re-creating a Polish state, as it would have been a direct affront to both Russia and Austria. He had previously re-constituted the Grand Duchy of Warsaw under the ruler of Saxony. Here Napoleon explains his decision to the Polish leaders.

Berthier, Murat and Rapp dine with Napoleon, 1812. The generals in charge of the 'Immense Army' included Murat, Ney and Davout, and many others who were not of the same high calibre. There was much personal rivalry, and they were only half-hearted about the campaign in Russia, vastly preferring to retire to their properties and their large personal fortunes. 'I can see, gentlemen, that you don't want to fight any longer', said Napoleon in a 'pep-talk' at Danzig.

Crossing the Niemen, June 1812. This event near Kovno really launched the Russian campaigns. The die was now cast: there could be no pulling back. There were no mountains or rough terrain, but physical obstacles in the shape of large wide rivers had to be overcome—and later of course there was the weather. The sheer size of the operation was a problem too; an army of over half a million men, with all arms and supplies, proved a ponderous force even to get on the move; and even Napoleon, no longer at the peak of his powers, had not tackled such a job before and he watched anxiously until all the troops were across.

Accepting this as a hostile act, and perhaps still prompted by dreams of eastern adventures based on Moscow, Napoleon decided on war against Russia in the summer of 1812: the scale of the venture, the size and nature of the resultant catastrophe, have caught the horrified imagination of generations since, and provided a theme for many writers.

Against a newly constituted Grande Armée of over 600,000 (mostly conscripts, and drawn from almost every land in Europe that Napoleon had over-run, as the best French troops were heavily committed in Spain), the Russian generals decided to withdraw, leading on the huge, motley and not easily manoeuvred cavalcade ever further into the relative wilderness of their vast country, without joining in pitched battles. Smolensk was taken in mid-August, and the French headed for Moscow, the capital. After a terribly destructive battle at Borodino, just west of Moscow, from which the defeated Russians retired in good order, Napoleon entered the capital on September 13, to find it largely deserted and in flames. The Russian 'scorched earth' policy was succeeding in denying food and even shelter to the invaders. There was nowhere to go except back to the west, and, after some hesitation, this began in October, with the Russian winter beginning and many hundreds of miles to be covered.

It was too late. The snow may not have been much earlier than usual, but it provided the final touches to the nightmare retreat back to the Niemen in early December, accomplished by considerably less than 20 per cent of those who had set out, ragged, half-starved, often bootless, almost overwhelmed by the blizzards that swept across the vast open spaces, where the only features in the landscape were the birch grove or

The Burning of Moscow. The occupation of the Czar's capital was to have been the prize for the Russian venture; but Kutuzov did not defend the city after the Battle of the Borodino, and Governor Rostopchin followed the traditional ruthless Russian 'scorched earth' policy. He evacuated the population, and groups of incendiarists started fires which destroyed huge areas, making the place untenable.

The Miseries of War, 1812. A few of the fortunate survivors trudge on, in improvised clothing, amid abandoned arms, equipment and the ever-present snow. The retreat from Moscow marked the real 'beginning of the end' for Napoleon's ambitions.

Napoleon leads his troops at Krasnoe, 1812. An incident in the Smolensk region during the retreat from Moscow: the 'little corporal' leads his grenadiers. 'Tip and run' tactics by Russian skirmishers, and threatening pincer-movements by larger groups of Kutuzov's men, often forced the French to turn and fight; and though the remnants of the Old Guard (with whom Napoleon had a special personal relationship) always acquitted themselves well, there was a steady loss of men, arms and baggage.

Napoleon's retreat from Moscow. He stayed with the remnants of his army until the Berezina had been crossed and Vilna reached. He had been deeply disturbed during the retreat by news of a plot in Paris to overthrow the Government, and, deciding that it would be bad for morale and efficiency if a long interval elapsed between news of his defeat and his return, he left the command to Murat and pushed on by the relatively speedy transport of a sledge, arriving in Paris on December 18.

pine-wood that gave cover to raiding Cossacks who, well-mounted, would whirl in with lance or sabre and quickly disappear before the dazed French troops could retaliate. Italian and Spanish conscripts suffered terribly, but there was no mutiny nor apparently any 'feeling' against Napoleon, while acts of high courage and discipline were known—notably the French engineers and sappers who worked for hours in the freezing waters of the Berezina to make pontoon bridges, and the gallant rearguard actions of Marshal Ney's troops in holding off the Russians. In spite of this nearly half a million men were left behind, either dead, wounded or missing.

One might feel that this was the end, and probably with everyone else it would have been. Napoleon, however, was still bent on preserving his hold on Central Europe. A desperate dash back to Paris and a lightning recruiting campaign saw him, in the space of four months, back in the field with a new army of untried young recruits who, at Lutzen and at Bautzen in Saxony, gained victories over a combined Prussian and Russian force. During the armistice which followed, he refused to compromise with Austrian demands, so that Austria, with a large army under

Surprise attack by Cossacks on Napoleon's troops at Brienne. After the Battle of Nations at Leipzig, the successful allies (Prussians, Russians and Austrians) pushed on westwards and invaded France itself. Napoleon aimed at keeping them divided and at Brienne in the Aube valley gained a victory over Blücher, thanks largely to the valour of the young recruits, the 'Maria-Louisa boys'. Other brilliant victories followed in the defence of Paris, but the allies' numbers were too great.

Schwarzenberg, took the side of the Allies. In spite of a further victory at Dresden, the toils were closing in, and a vast enveloping movement by Russian, Prussian and Austrian armies, with their respective sovereigns in attendance, brought Napoleon to face them outside Leipzig in October 1813—his army depleted, himself for once undecided on the best course. Beaten and routed at this three-day 'Battle of Nations', he retired to France, leaving the various German states to assert their independence. Even then, however, he would not accept defeat, but, refusing to treat with the Allies, organised with all his old skill and resources a series of victories in the Seine and Marne region against the fore-runners of the main invading forces. However, he could not get back to Paris in time to check another thrust, so retired to Fontainebleau to await events. Paris capitulated, most public leaders (even the faithful marshals) were for giving up the struggle, so on April 6, 1814 Napoleon renounced the thrones of France and Italy, and accepted banishment to the island of Elba off the Italian coast. The Bourbons were back in the person of Louis XVIII.

Still the story had not ended: some sovereigns 'take an unconscionable

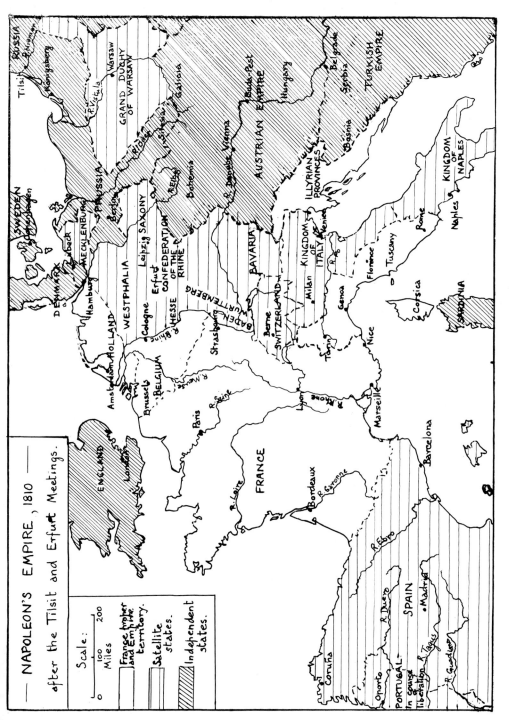

— NAPOLEON'S EMPIRE, 1810 —
after the Tilsit and Erfurt Meetings.

Scale:
0   100   200
Miles

France proper
and Empire
territory.

Satellite
states.

Independent
states.

Envoy from Paris, February 23, 1814. The allied armies had crossed
the Rhine into French territory in December 1813—Prussians under
Blücher, Austrians under Schwarzenberg, with Czar Alexander and many
Russians. Napoleon had his back to the wall—his troops outnumbered,
his marshals divided on the advisability of continuing the struggle, the
populace of Paris uncertain. To a suggestion of surrender sent from Paris
he replied, 'If I am to be scourged, let the whip at least come on me of
necessity and not through any voluntary stooping of my own'. In several
engagements in the valleys of the Seine, Marne and Aube, he showed
all his old skill against allied detachments; but he could not be in the
capital at the same time, and he had not the men to risk a confrontation
against the total army strength of the allies, who entered Paris on
March 31.

Farewell at the Tuileries. Napoleon's mental anguish on leaving his comrades in arms, en route to exile in Elba, was acute; he could not foresee his triumphant return to the Tuileries Palace a few months later.

time a-dying'—though not always in quite the sense that Charles II had used the phrase.

After ten months on Elba, Napoleon returned, landed on the Riviera coast, and with less than 1,000 men, journeyed across the French Alps and eastern France to Paris, gaining support and kindling enthusiasm with

OPPOSITE: 'I alone am representative of the people'. After defeat at the Battle of Nations at Leipzig in 1813, Napoleon returned to France still bent on carrying on the struggle. In spite of his appeal for national unity, he encountered strong opposition among the deputies of the national assembly, and early in 1814 dissolved the legislative body, accusing them of lack of faith: 'What is the throne itself? Four preces of gilded wood covered with velvet? No, a throne is a man and I am that man, with my will, my character and my fame!'

ABOVE: Napoleon's Residence on Elba, 1814. His banishment to Elba was not accompanied by the austerities of St Helena; he was in effect the King or overlord of the island, with a palace at Portoferrajo and the Villa of San Martino, along with a minute army and a grant of money for upkeep. BELOW: Napoleon returns from Elba. As his ship approaches Cannes on the Riviera coast, having dodged patrolling cruisers, Napoleon eagerly scans the horizon, while his 'staff' keep under cover.

Napoleon greated by his troops on return from Elba. Napoleon admitted later that he came back as an adventurer, with eleven hundred men (largely from the Old Guard) who had remained loyal to him. He began the Hundred Days by a mountain march via Castellane, Digne and Gap towards Grenoble, and at the Laffrey Pass the battalion sent to halt his progress acclaimed him as their emperor, waving their shakos on the end of their muskets. After this emotional moment his progress was swift and sure, and he fast gathered more support.

every mile. This final episode, the famous Hundred Days, or the 'Cent Jours' as it is known in France, makes one of the most marvellous true-life stories of all time. Napoleon's career ended, as it began, with all the characteristics of a romantic novel.

Always popular with soldiers and peasantry, in spite of everything, Napoleon's acceptance and resumption of power were made easier by the mistakes and dismal insufficiences of the restored Bourbon government; —its toleration of 'émigrés', its retrenchment of the army. He had only to represent himself as liberal and republican in sympathy, but unfortunately

Louis XVIII leaves Paris ahead of Napoleon. During Napoleon's exile on Elba, the Bourbons had been restored in the person of Louis XVIII. When Napoleon's triumphant return had brought him to Fontainebleau, by March 19, Louis decided to leave Paris, and departed at midnight by coach for Flanders.

pushed towards autocracy by the exigencies of war, to win over the waverers. He hoped to sow dissension among the Allies, whose leaders, already meeting in Vienna, had been thrown into confusion by his melo-dramatic return; they refused to accept Napoleon's protestations of peace and non-aggression, bound themselves to continue the struggle, and put a large army in the field—a mixed force, chiefly British, under Wellington, and a Prussian army under Blücher. With an army that was smaller but largely made up of enthusiasts and veterans, Napoleon went to meet them in Belgium, hoping for a victory before the Russians and Austrians could add their strength. It would be unfair to call this 'the gambler's last throw', even though, with age and success, Napoleon had become more apt to take a chance. Yet even had he succeeded at Water-loo, his success would only have been temporary; the continent was inflamed against him, the middle classes in France itself wanted an end to the perpetual campaigning now that it was clearly seen to be the result of personal ambition rather than zeal to protect France's frontiers and safeguard the Revolution. As it was, age, strain and reverses had taken their toll on Napoleon's decisiveness and confidence. He had begun the short campaign brilliantly, with a victory on June 16 at Ligny over Blücher's Prussians; but at the field of Waterloo on Sunday the 18th, there were errors in staff-work, unaccustomed slowness in recon-naissance and intelligence, and a reluctance to commit his crack troops, the Old Guard, until it was too late. In spite of a terrific artillery bom-bardment and a series of cavalry charges, the steadfastness of the mixed

Presentation of Eagles and Standards. During the Hundred Days, Napoleon made many liberal concessions, and appears to have been prepared for the role of constitutional monarch; but he stepped up military preparedness in the face of antagonism from the rest of Europe and the reconstitution of the Imperial Guard was central to his plans. At a magnificent ceremony on June 1, 1815—the so-called Champ de Mai—Napoleon, attired in his coronation finery, whipped up immense enthusiasm for the Empire by himself taking the oath to observe the constitution, and by distributing flags and symbols to the Imperial Guard in a style that was reminiscent of ancient Rome.

Napoleon at Waterloo. June 18, 1815. Defeat is not far off. Hesitancy had never marked his decisions on the field of battle; but having waited for hours for reinforcements from de Grouchy, and having reluctantly and belatedly committed his crack troops, the Old Guard, Napoleon has nothing left to satisfy the entreaties of his field commanders.

British, Dutch, Belgian and German lines brilliantly commanded by Wellington, prevailed, and the arrival late in the day of the supposedly retreating Prussians finally settled the issue. The excitement of the Hundred Days was nearly over: back in Paris on June 22 Napoleon finally abdicated and was taken aboard the British warship *Bellerophon* at Roche-

ABOVE: Defeated in the field at Waterloo the French regiments retreat towards Paris, taking their wounded comrades in what transport they could muster—here a commandeered or hired farm cart complete, apparently, with its owner.

fort. The *Northumberland*, to which he was transferred, reached St Helena in 70 days, and there he died after six years of exile, in 1821. It was typical of him that, having missed the fitting end of death on the field of battle and having now to relinquish the sword, he took up the pen, marshalling words and arguments, truths and falsehoods, as he had once marshalled men to do his will.

BELOW: A last glimpse for the ex-Emperor of the ship which brought him into exile at St Helena, his momentous career at last terminated.

8: Retrospect

NOW, nearly 160 years after the carnage and the smoke of countless battlefields is long forgotten, one is prompted to ask: What was achieved? What came out of all the bloodshed and destruction? What must be our verdict on the man whose ambition gave rise to it all? The degree of condemnation has not proved as great as might have been expected— strangely perhaps at first sight, though not so strangely if an objective assessment is attempted, and things are reviewed relative to their time. Of course, during the struggle against Britain, he was 'that man', 'the Corsican ogre'. Yet not half a century later he could appear as the hero of more than one poem by Browning, and there must have been thousands of Victorian homes whose walls carried pictures of him: the weary French sentry, having slept at his post, awakens to find that Napoleon, on his rounds, stands on guard with the abandoned musket: 'C'est

Napoleon's residence on St Helena. The rather shabby old mansion of Longwood was Napoleon's island-prison from 1815 until his death in 1821. It had few amenities, and Napoleon undoubtedly suffered from the inactivity, lack of privacy, and dissensions among his small household staff. One favourite occupation was gardening.

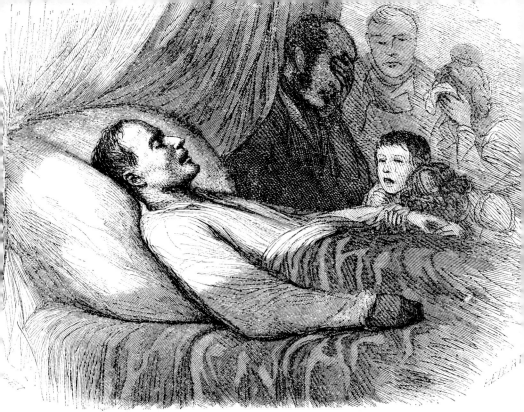

Death of Napoleon. After nearly six years of exile on lonely St Helena, living a life of galling inactivity and restraint with a small household at Longwood, and never again seeing his wife or his son, Napoleon died, probably from the effects of a cancerous ulcer, aggravated by a long-standing liver complaint. Denied a warrior's death on the field of battle, he yet showed his quality by spending his last days recording his genuine gratitude and concern for all who had helped him in his career.

l'Empéreur!', or the Grenadier, dying by the wayside in the retreat from Moscow, half rises from the snow to salute the hunched figure that rides grimly by—sentimental, of course, but significant.

One does not have to repeat the adulation of convinced Bonapartists to admit that Napoleon had remarkable qualities as a leader of men. It was almost inevitable that, in a life so crammed with incident, and driven as he was by a consuming, compulsive energy that made him in turn an Alexander, Hannibal, Caesar, Charlemagne, he should have coun-tenanced many crimes, and should be open to the charge of 'man of blood' that can be made against all military leaders (and many civilian ones). Everything about him was larger than life; he had immense per-sonal magnetism, could make ordinary people look beyond the common-

Napoleon's coffin brought back to France. The frigate Belle Poule *brought Napoleon's remains from St Helena back to France in 1840, and the journey was made in the style and dignity proper to a great occasion. Napoleon had originally been buried on the island. When exhumed his body was found to be in an excellent state of preservation. He was dressed in his old uniform.*

place of everyday, and his soldiers adored him: from raw recruit to haughty marshal he was to them 'the little corporal'. Of course, there was deterioration with age and success: pictures of him in middle age compared unfavourably with the keen young commander at the bridge of Arcola, and one regrets the something that was lost on the way. Yet there is no denying that he left a legend, a legend that inspired France (and others) at the time and for long years after. He praised hard work and believed in efficiency, and gave to common people and common soldiers an ideal of glory that raised them above themselves: one could wish that a leader so gifted could have realised that conquest was not the ultimate way of winning the hearts of men.

With a personality so out of the ordinary, and a career so crowded, generalisation is perhaps dangerous: sneers and adulation are apt to rebound! Undoubtedly he was a tyrant, yet his claim to be 'the child of the Revolution' is equally true. His attempt to justify himself by 're-touching history' during his exile on St Helena can be shrugged aside; but many of his sayings have become almost proverbial, and we probably unconsciously quote him as often as we quote Shakespeare.

There can be no argument, however, over the importance of the period 1789 to 1815, for France, Europe and the world. In making his bid during this bridge period between the 18th and 19th centuries, Napoleon set his stamp on the crowded, eventful, war-torn years in such a far-ranging,

Napoleon's funeral at Les Invalides. The re-burial was not merely a matter of pomp and circumstance. Although some people at the time, 1840, thought that the return was politically inadvisable, yet there can be little doubt that the ceremonies were prompted by genuine regard for a great man. They proved the strength of the 'Napoleonic legend'.

Napoleon's magnificent funeral carriage at the procession preceding the burial service.

forceful way that they make a necessary introduction to all that has happened since. Every period, of course, is both a culmination of past periods and a starting-point for new. Much that he did certainly closed the book on the relics of medievalism in western Europe; he showed up the weaknesses, the pettiness and shabbiness of the 'ancien régime'. Equally, much that he did, or at any rate much that he preached even if he did not practise, was conceived in the spirit of a new age, and the 19th century was to owe as much on its political side to French 'Liberty, Equality, Fraternity' as it was on its economic side to British technology and industrial organisation.

In fact, in his 20 years of power, Napoleon's career and activities touched on almost everything that was to shake or shape the world that followed; autocracy and democracy, imperialism and independence, free trade, and protection, colonialism, slavery, the rights of man and the rights of nations. For these reasons, as well as for the practical judicial and administrative reforms that lasted so long, and the feeling of glory or glamour that his name evoked in the minds of French people for generations, it can be said that the Napoleonic Period lasted long after 1815. Ironically enough, some of his most important achievements and results proved to be the unintentional ones—notably the growth of nationalist feeling in many lands that really brought about his ultimate downfall; and doubly ironically, nobody is more responsible for laying the

Napoleon's Tomb in Paris. England had required him to be buried on St Helena, and for nearly twenty years his body occupied a simple grave under a blank head-stone, guarded by one sentry in the little Geranium Valley which had been his favourite walk. In 1840, however, the English government deferred to French wishes, and his remains were returned to Paris, to be buried with honour in the Invalides. The symbolic significance of this event appealed to many people besides the French. This print shows officers paying homage at the new tomb immediately after the interment.

foundations of modern Germany than Napoleon! By his humiliation of Austria he threw the smaller German states into the arms of Prussia, and by the stinging defeat of Prussia at Jena he provoked forces that led to such a regeneration of that state that its world-wide effects are still working themselves out. Even a Napoleon cannot regulate all events; yet he did achieve so much, and proved on so many occasions that Britain has had less worthy enemies, that one is impelled into a measure of agreement with the English schoolboy's assessment of him: 'A great chap in many ways; pity he couldn't have been on our side!'

Appendix 1: Chronology of Events

1760　The Industrial Revolution in Britain—inventions (water-powered) in textile industries.

1762　'Le Contrat Social' by J.-J. Rousseau.

1769　Birth of Napoleon, Wellington and Ney.

1776　American Declaration of Independence.

1776　'The Wealth of Nations' by Adam Smith.

1778　Death of Voltaire.

1784　Ministry of William Pitt, the younger.

1785　Cartwright's Power Loom heralds steam-driven machinery.

1788　Capt. Phillip lands in New South Wales—the beginning of Australia.

1789　French Revolution—Fall of the Bastille.

1792　France declared a republic.

1792　'The Rights of Man' by Tom Paine.

1793　France at War in Europe.

1793　Reign of Terror in France. Napoleon at Toulon.

1794　The Ordnance Survey begins work on the first 1 inch maps in South-East England.

1795　Napoleon restores order in Paris.

1795　The Speenhamland Edict—poor law supplement to wages from the rates.

1796　Napoleon's marriage to Josephine de Beauharnais.

1796　First North Italian Campaign.

1797　Peace of Campo Formio with Austria.

1797　Partition of Poland between Russia, Prussia and Austria.

1798　'Essay on Population' by Rev. Malthus.

1798　Napoleon's Egyptian and Syrian Campaign.

1798　Nelson's victory at Aboukir Bay.

1799　Coup d'état at St Cloud—Napoleon First Consul.

1800　Second North Italian Campaign—battle of Marengo.

1800　Battle of Hohenlinden—Peace of Lunéville.

1801　Nelson at Copenhagen.

1801　First Census in Britain, now acknowledged 'Workshop of the World'.

1801　Act of Union—one parliament for United Kingdom of Great Britain and Ireland.

1801　Romantic Movement in English literature under way—the Lakeland poets.

1802　Treaty of Amiens.

1802　Napoleon Consul for Life.

1802　Napoleon's Concordat with Catholic Church.

1802   First Factory Act in Britain.

1802   William Cobbett started 'Political Register'.

1803   War resumed.

1804   Napoleon's Civil Code revises judicial and legal system.

1804   Other 'home' reforms in France—rejuvenation of Paris.

1804   France an hereditary empire—Napoleon crowns himself.

1804   Plans for Invasion—'la Grande Armée'.

1804   Execution of the Duc d'Enghien.

1804   Pitt's last Ministry.

1805   Nelson's victory at Trafalgar.

1805   French victories at Ulm and Austerlitz—Treaty of Schönbrunn.

1806   Holy Roman Empire abolished, limiting Austrian influence—replaced by Confederation of the Rhine.

1806   French victories at Jena and Auerstadt against Prussia—Berlin Decree prohibits trade with Britain.

1807   Act making slavery illegal, after agitation by Wilberforce.

1807   Battles of Eylau and Friedland—Peace of Tilsit between Napoleon and Czar Alexander.

1807   British Orders in Council, aiming at strict blockade of France and supporters.

1807   Milan Decree of Napoleon, aimed at all shipping having any contact with Britain.

1808   Napoleon replaces Charles IV of Spain by his brother Joseph.

1808   French defeat at Baylen in south Spain.

1808   Peninsular War begins—landing of British troops in Portugal under Wellesley.

1808   Napoleon reaches Madrid—Sir John Moore's retreat to Corunna.

1809   French victories against Austrians at Ratisbon and later at Wagram—Peace of Vienna.

1809   Battle of Talavera—Wellesley made Duke of Wellington.

1810   Battle of Busaco and defence of the lines of Torres Vedras.

1810   Napoleon divorces Josephine and marries Maria Louisa.

1811   Birth of a son, the 'King of Rome', to Napoleon and Maria Louisa.

1811   French finally driven out of Portugal.

1812   Wellington's successes at Ciudad Rodrigo and Badajoz, and Battle of Salamanca.

1812   Napoleon's Russian campaign—Battle of the Borodino and Retreat from Moscow.

1813   Wellington's victories at Vitoria and San Sebastian.

1813   French victories at Lützen, Bautzen and Dresden.

1813   Napoleon defeated by combined Austrians, Russians and Prussians at Leipzig, 'the Battle of Nations'.

1813   Steam navigation on the Clyde.

1814   British occupy Toulouse in south-west France.

1814   Napoleon banished to Elba—return of the Bourbons to Paris.

1815 Napoleon's return from Elba—the 'Hundred Days'.

1815 Allied leaders meeting at Vienna find Napoleon's peace proposals unacceptable.

1815 Battle of Waterloo—success for Wellington and the Allies.

1815 Abdication of Napoleon—exile on St Helena—Bourbons again restored in Paris—Congress of Vienna wound up with plans for further meetings.

1816 Luddite riots in Britain.

1819 'Peterloo Massacre' following years of social distress and disturbances.

1821 Death of Napoleon on St Helena.

1820-40 Years of scattered political and nationalist outbreaks in Europe; of social distress, material progress (coming of the railways) and political agitation and reform (Parliament, local government, factories, Poor Law) in Britain; and of the re-entry of France into the life of Europe (with a more constitutional monarchy after 1830, the beginnings of an Industrial Revolution, and a vigorous Romantic movement in literature).

1840 Return of Napoleon's body to France.

1852 Napoleon's nephew, after election as president, assumed supreme power following a coup d'état and proclaimed himself Emperor Napoleon III.

Appendix 2: Some books for further reading

The Age of Napoleon, J. C. Herold (Horizon).

Wellington in the Peninsular, Jac Weller (Vane).

Life and Times of Napoleon (Hamlyn).

Years of the Sword, E. Longford (Pan).

Regiments at Waterloo, R. North (Almark).

Soldiers of the Peninsular War, R. North (Almark).

French Napoleonic Artillery, M. Head (Almark).

Foot Regiments of the Imperial Guard, M. Head (Almark).

The Prussian Army, 1809-1815, D. Nash (Almark).